A YEAR FULL OF
FLOWERS

A YEAR FULL OF FLOWERS

FRESH IDEAS TO BRING FLOWERS INTO YOUR LIFE EVERY DAY

JIM McCANN AND JULIE McCANN MULLIGAN

WITH BO NILES

RODALE

Produced by The Philip Lief Group, Inc.

Copyright © 2004 by 800-FLOWERS, INC.

Photographs
© 800-FLOWERS, INC., pp. 2, 8, 10, 11, 12, 13, 14, 15, 18, 23, 25, 52, 55, 59, 90, 94, 104-105, 106, 107, 108, 109, 154-155, 156, 157, 159, 188, 200, 201, 202, 203, 240, 244, 249, 252, 253.

© The Philip Lief Group, Inc., pp. 16-17, 28, 32, 44, 86, 98, 101, 102, 103, 110, 114, 128, 132, 136, 140, 144, 150, 152, 184, 192, 195, 224, 228, 232, 236, 247, 248, 254-260 and all instructional photographs.

© Maria Ferrari pp. 22, 46, 47, 48, 56-57, 58, 62, 66, 70, 74, 78, 82, 118, 122, 148, 149, 158, 160, 164, 168, 172, 176, 180, 204, 208, 212, 216, 220, 250.

Printed in the United States of America
Rodale Inc. makes every effort to use acid-free ∞, recycled paper ♺.

Book design by Annie Jeon

Library of Congress Cataloging-in-Publication Data

McCann, Jim, date.
    A year full of flowers: fresh ideas to bring flowers into your life every day/ Jim McCann and Julie McCann Mulligan, with Bo Niles.
        p.   cm
    Includes index.
    ISBN 1–57954–904–7 paperback
    1. Flower arrangement.   2. Floral decorations.   3. Flowers.   4. Handicraft.
    I. Mulligan, Julie McCann.   II. Niles, Bo.   III. Title.
    SB449.M26   2004
    745.92—dc22   2004014491

Distributed to the trade by Holtzbrinck Publishers

2 4 6 8 10 9 7 5 3 1   paperback

ACKNOWLEDGMENTS

The McCann family embodies "family business" in the truest sense of the term. Our company, 1-800-FLOWERS.COM, wouldn't be as successful, gratifying, or even possible, without contributions from almost every member of our family. Some work full time for the company, and others, such as our wonderful sister Peggy and our very special brother Kevin, help out on holidays and whenever else they are needed.

At home, each of us has been lucky enough to have the never-ending support of our spouses and children.

From Jim: To my family, Marylou, Erin, James, and Matthew, for understanding that being in a business that helps people express themselves and connect to the important people in their lives does not always leave sufficient time for our own expressions and connections to the degree that we would like.

From Julie: With all my love and thanks to my husband, Jimmy, for always believing in me and encouraging me to follow my dreams. And to my children, Shane, Meggie, and Casey, for making my life complete and always being proud of what I do.

While our family has done so much to help make 1-800-FLOWERS® a success, we'd also like to thank the people who worked on the book and helped create something that truly reflects our company:

Judy Capodanno, who believed in this book for many years and never gave up on it.

Margot Schupf, at Rodale, who had the vision to know that these ideas would make a wonderful book and then made it happen!

Ken Young, for his patience and persistence in working out the details.

Bo Niles, for putting the ideas into words and making each project easy to follow.

Maria Ferrari, for our years of friendship and collaboration and her beautiful photographs and dedication to her craft.

Joe and Mary Van Blerck, who brought us into the digital age. From the basic step-by-step photography to the excitement of capturing the sun as it shone through a poppy, you are both always a pleasure to work with. Your professionalism, talent, hard work, and dedication are much appreciated.

The best photography team ever: Jose Gutierrez, floral designer, set builder, and jack of all trades; Laraine D. Elia, our stylist who is great at finding whatever is needed to make the project just right and is a fellow collector; and Teresa Madtes, our production manager who makes sure we all stay on track and does whatever it takes to get the job done. We'd also like to thank her for close to 40 fabulous years of friendship and support.

contents

FOREWORD

Flowers make people feel good—that's why I love them. Everybody does. Flowers help us celebrate meaningful moments in our lives. They help us connect with each other, whether it's to bring a smile or dry a tear. Flowers say things we may not be able to find the right words for. They bring out the best in us. That's why, after more than 25 years as a florist, I still love my job. Every day, I'm able to help people connect with one another in big ways and small, through the gift of flowers.

I grew up in a family that loved flowers. When I was in my twenties, I purchased my first flower shop. Within 10 years, the company had expanded to be a chain of shops in and around New York City. Then, in 1986, I learned of an opportunity that I couldn't resist: to buy a company that had the toll-free number, 1-800-FLOWERS. The thought was to select a group of the very best, most talented, and caring florists in each town in the country and give them all the same telephone number. What a wonderful concept—one that became even more so with the invention of the World Wide Web. We became 1-800-FLOWERS.COM®. Now that, to me, was a magical idea!

I love what I do, but, of course, there's no way I could do it alone. That's where our Bloomnet® florist partners come in, making our arrangements of flowers for us now around the world. I've discovered over the years that I have a fortunate knack

bloomnet®
basics

Our Bloomnet® florists are the elite of the industry, representing the top 10 percent of all florists in the U.S. Over the past 25 years, 1-800-FLOWERS.COM has combed the nation to build a highly selective network of participating members who share our passion for helping people connect and express themselves. Each member is carefully chosen based on their talent, capability, and commitment to customer service. They represent the leaders in floral artistry, providing our customers with the highest quality, most beautifully designed floral arrangements supported by our unique fulfillment and delivery capabilities.

for finding creative people to work for me, and our Bloomnet® florists prove that every day. The creative environment in the 1-800-FLOWERS® team allows our members to flourish and to create the best of the best in gift products for our customers.

Every step of the way, I couldn't imagine working without the creative input from not just the Bloomnet® team, but also my family. My brother, Chris McCann, runs the daily operations of the company; my sister, Julie McCann Mulligan, is our creative director. Julie loves to inspire people to get in touch with their creative side—through flowers, of course! Julie often speaks at flower shows and design workshops around the country and has appeared on numerous TV shows. Perhaps you've seen or met her. She loves to show people how to use flowers in their lives. She loves to see people connect through flowers.

In this book, we will be sharing some of the wonder and magic flowers can bring into your life. People need to put their arms around their flowers—psychologically speaking, I believe—by personalizing them. Not only flowers they pick or purchase themselves, but also flowers they may receive as a gift. Maybe you want to change out a flower or two; maybe you want to exchange the vase for another, more personal kind of container. Anything goes in nature. Anything goes with flowers, too. You'll see. As my sister says, "Just have fun with it!®" I, for one, am sure you will.

Tim McCann

INTRODUCTION

You can buy almost any flower you want at any time of year—not only through a toll-free number like ours, by mail order, or on line, but also, in many cases, at your neighborhood florist, as well as at venues as diverse as your corner grocery, farmer's market, or nursery. With so many flowers to choose from, from so many places, it's no wonder we want to gather up armfuls of flowers and bring them home.

Then what?

At 1-800-FLOWERS®, we don't think you can ever make a mistake arranging flowers. There are so many ways to display and enjoy flowers that we can hardly count them all! For example, you can mass one type of flower—such as tulips or peonies—in one gorgeous vase. You can place a stem or two of a fabulously colorful flower like gerbera daisy in each of a series of small bottles and set them all out in a row on a windowsill, or here and there on a table, or throughout your house wherever you like. You can float some pretty blossoms in a teacup, ceramic pie plate, or bowl. Dry some stems and blooms and hang them on a ceiling beam or a rack on the wall, or press some petals in a book or journal.

Create an arrangement inspired by the projects in this book.

Or all of the above!

When you look at our catalogs and log onto our Web site, you'll notice that we often don't tell you exactly what each and every single flower will be in the final arrangement that you—or someone in another part of the country—may order. That's because we like to have our Bloomnet® family—the florists whom we've invited to collaborate with us— feel free to improvise, if they have to, if and when a particular flower happens not to be at its peak at that particular moment. We trust our florists to make and deliver beautiful arrangements that look as true to our photographs as possible. And with this book, we trust

that you will do beautiful things with flowers, too.

Just as we do with our Bloomnet® family, this book presents you with a number of projects—34, in fact— and recipes to follow, including the amounts of flowers you'll need and tools you need for each. Some flowers are specified as "stems," because certain varieties feature multiple sprigs or blossoms on each stem. The amounts we specify, therefore, may not be absolutely precise, because some stems may have more sprigs or blooms than others. To be on the safe side, buy more stems than you need—that way you can choose the best blooms and cut accordingly.

We also offer some general information on choosing and preparing your flowers and containers, plus some design fundamentals, and tips about taking care of your flower arrangements that will make working with flowers fun and easy and help keep your flowers healthy longer.

The most important thing about flowers, though, is this: Most flowers can be arranged any way you like! So don't feel you have to slavishly duplicate what we've done here, flower by flower. We'd much rather you look at our projects for inspiration—and then create your own version with whatever flowers you like, in

whatever container pleases you. It's no big deal if you change out some of the flowers we've shown you for others you like better. It's no big deal if you want to use a container that looks nothing like the one we happened to choose for our photo. Look around your house, search your garage or attic, or even check out flea markets. You probably own lots of objects that can be converted into potential containers. Most of the time, if it can hold water, it can hold flowers.

Finally, our step-by-steps are structured to be easy to follow, but you can adjust a step or two if you don't want to end up making an arrangement that looks like a flower-by-flower copy of ours. Each project is tagged with its level of difficulty and amount of time

it will take to complete. Most take only minutes to make. A few projects require more flowers and, therefore, take a bit longer. At 1-800-FLOWERS®, we believe that arranging flowers should be easy and comfortable—and fun. Fun is our motto. Let it be yours, too.

Just have fun with it!®

Julie M°Cann Mulligan

and the 1-800-FLOWERS® family

basics

choosing flowers

Every flower is a soul blossoming in Nature.

—Gerard de Nerval

Choosing flowers is an adventure! Flowers—like people—have different personalities, shapes, and styles, so pick what appeals to you on any given day—or, if your flowers are going to be a gift, pick what suits the lucky recipient. What we love to do—and suggest you do, too—is simply check out whatever happens to be blooming in the garden at the moment or what's in stock at the local flower shop or farmer's market. If you're looking for something specific and can't seem to locate it right away, you should be able to find what you want through a mail-order resource or online.

in the garden

If you have a cutting garden, you are lucky indeed! Growing your own flowers gives you complete control over how and when you cut them, plus you have the satisfaction of knowing you've nurtured them along the way. It's always best to cut flowers early in the morning, just after the dew evaporates, or late in the afternoon when the sun is just about to set, because hot sun can hasten wilting. Use the sharpest florist's scissors or pruning shears possible. Blunt blades may damage stems. Carrying a bucket of tepid water out to the garden is a good idea, too. As you cut your flowers, you can give them a quick, refreshing drink—and they can stay in the bucket until you're ready to work with them. A bucket's the easiest way to carry them inside, too.

at the florist

If you don't have a garden, there are lots of other places where you can find fresh flowers, such as nurseries, roadside stands, and farmer's markets—even grocery stores. You'll probably find the greatest selection at your local flower shops, though, because stocking flowers, after all, is their business. It's great fun to shop around and see what's available. Many florists nowadays go to great lengths to bring you the finest, freshest flowers in season; many import flowers from abroad, too. So, even if you want to bring your mom or best girlfriend a bouquet of tulips in November, don't fret! Check your florist or look online. You'll probably be able to buy or order exactly what she wants.

Most florists receive shipments of flowers at least three times a week, if not more. At busy times of year, especially around holidays such as Christmas, Valentine's Day, or Mother's Day, they'll receive packages of fresh flowers every day. When flowers arrive at the shop, they are immediately transferred to buckets of cool water to rehydrate them after their journey. After inspecting every flower for freshness, the florist discards any that look as if they are beginning to deteriorate. To prepare his healthy flowers for sale, the florist starts a process called conditioning. Conditioning strengthens the flower stems so that they will be more receptive to taking up food—in the form of floral food or preservative—and water.

Quick tips

- Unless you need a particular variety of flowers for a specific reason, buy what's blooming. The quality is usually better and the price is right!
- When choosing flowers, look for flowers at their peak—firm, succulent, and not discolored along their edges.

To help flowers absorb nutrient-enriched water, the florist slices off the bottom inch of each stem, at a 45-degree angle, under water. This cut exposes more of the pith that lies under the skin of the stem to water than if it were cut straight across. Next, he removes all leaves (and buds) that would lie under the water line in the bucket. Waterlogged leaves rot quickly, which hastens the deterioration of the entire flower. After changing out the old, cool water for fresh, tepid water (plus floral preservative), most flowers are placed in a cooler kept at a more-or-less constant 34 to 38 degrees so that they will not open prematurely. Tropical flowers may be maintained at a slightly warmer 50 degrees or—depending upon the species—at room temperature. Ideally, the flower shop is fairly cool and humid.

timing your blooms

No matter where you buy your flowers, you should thoroughly inspect each stem or bunch of flowers you like before making your purchase. Unless you plan on displaying your flowers the same day you buy them—or you don't care how long they'll last in your arrangement—your flowers should display blooms that have not opened completely. Leaves should look firm and bright and green. Curled or discolored edges are a sure sign that the leaf—and flower—will not last long.

Quick tip

Flowers tend to open at different speeds, so if you are planning a special event such as a graduation party or birthday, you can always call your florist shop ahead of time to be sure the flowers you'd like to use in your arrangements will open in time and be at their peak.

When you are choosing flowers with multiple blossoms, be sure to look for ones that have blooms in various stages of readiness—including plump buds that look as if they're just about to pop open. That way, you'll know that your flowers will keep on blooming as long as you want them to. If buds are hard and green, they probably won't open.

color

When choosing flowers, you'll probably be guided by color, then by shape and texture. Color is usually what makes the first impression. Color invites you into an arrangement. Color also sends out emotional cues. Think of the exuberant red of a carnation or bird-of-paradise; the cheerful yellows and oranges of sunflowers, marigolds, and gerbera daisies; the tender peaches and pinks of roses and peonies; and the romance of lavender-blue lilac and hydrangea.

If you have ever flipped through color chips in a paint store, you know that there are literally thousands of colors you can choose from. Same with flowers! Painters and designers learn about color (and print up color chips) by referring to what's known as a "color wheel," which is based, like a rainbow, on six colors— red, orange, yellow, green, blue, and purple—and the various tones, tints, and shades that link them. Some

colors contrast with each other: red with green, say, or orange with blue, or yellow with purple. Others seem to merge or blend: purple with lavender, orange with salmon, yellow with ivory.

The simplest way to remember how color works is to think of colors in families: red with red-orange and orange, for example, or pink-violet-blue, or yellow-to-peach.

FRESH
thoughts®

Color and mood are companions in design. Here are the six basic colors and the moods they inspire. Consider them singly and in combination when you make your choice of flowers. Mixing flowers that connote different feelings is one way to personalize your arrangement and make it fresh and inviting.

	red	intense, stimulating	passionate
	orange	fiery, vibrant	exuberant
	yellow	radiant, inviting	thoughtful
	green	refreshing, pacifying	serene
	blue	peaceful, soothing	tranquil
	violet	moody, seductive	romantic

The most harmonious flower arrangements tend to fall within a narrow range of colors in a single family, but that doesn't mean you have to makes yours in the same way. In nature, anything goes in terms of mixing and blending colors, shapes, and textures. You can put together any flowers in any way that suits you, too. Just remember that nature has an enormous canvas to paint on: the whole world! A flower arrangement may be nature in miniature, but your room is not a microcosm of the whole world.

Since color makes such an impact, ask yourself two "colorful" questions before you go to the florist: One, do you want your flowers to coordinate with the décor of the room (or tabletop) that they are intended for—or would you prefer that the colors stand out from their setting? And two, do you want the colors of your flowers to coordinate with each other—or do you want them to strike a dramatic contrast, one bloom with the next? To heighten the drama of a display, for instance, a contrasting color may be used to "spot" and set off the main color family; consider, for example, how a few dark raspberry-red roses spotted throughout a blush-peach-salmon-cream bouquet will pop out and make the bouquet sing.

shape and texture

Flowers assume a variety of shapes. Most fall into one of four categories: spherical or round, like giant allium, viburnum, or hydrangea; spiked, like spirea, lavender, or heather; domed, like certain types of chrysanthemum; or starlike, like asters, daisies, and sunflowers. Not every flower, of course, fits the categories. Some, like baby's breath, are frothy. Others exhibit dramatic, idiosyncratic shapes; examples of these include bird-of-paradise and calla lilies. Trumpet or bell-like flowers include the tulip, daffodil, amaryllis, and bells of Ireland. Delicate flowers such as anemones or nasturtiums have only a few fragile petals, while denser flowers, such as delphinium or stephanotis, and some orchids, cluster several blossoms along one stalk.

Texture is what gives a floral arrangement its sense of energy. Flowers and leaves can appear rough or coarse, like those of a globe artichoke, or they may look fluffy, like Queen Anne's lace. They may be glossy, like some varieties of tulip, boxwood, and magnolia leaves. Or, they may be delicate. Or sturdy. It's fun to combine flowers and leaves with different textures—the frothy with the shiny, for example, or flowers bearing multiple blooms with ones that have only a single flowerhead. It's up to you!

flower shapes

spherical   spiked   domed   starlike

leaves, greens, moss, grass, and evergreens

Foliage comes in many forms. First, of course, there are the leaves on the flowers you've selected for your arrangement. Then, there are leafy green plants, such as ferns, ivy, and palms. Other options include asparagus fern, plain and seeded eucalyptus, magnolia, lemon leaves, and pittosporum nigra. Yet another option is moss. Florists rely on several types of moss to achieve a naturalistic effect. These include sheet moss, sphagnum moss, reindeer moss, and Spanish moss. Mosses range in color from bright green to gray. Wheat grass is a current favorite with florists, who plant it in flats or other containers to be admired alone or "plant" it with flowers inserted in the grass, as if in a lawn. Finally, during the December holidays, evergreens such as fir, cedar, pine, spruce, and holly are often used as the foundation for a floral display—or on their own.

assorted leaves and greens

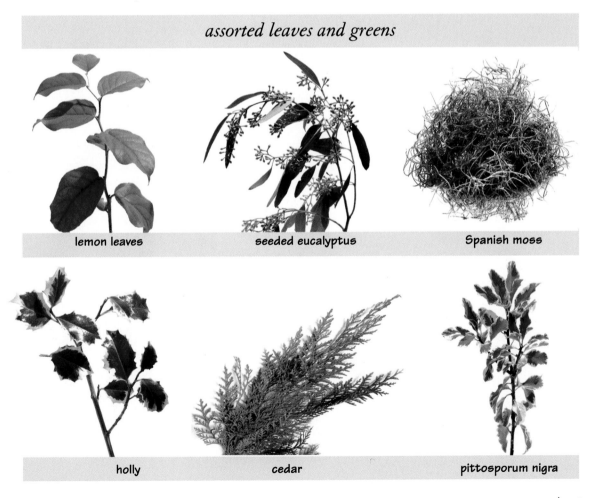

lemon leaves

seeded eucalyptus

Spanish moss

holly

cedar

pittosporum nigra

conditioning
flowers

Correct handling of flowers refines the personality.

—Bokuyo Takeda

Conditioning flowers is easy to do and well worth the extra few minutes it takes to get flowers ready before arranging them in any way. When you condition flowers, you basically follow the same steps the florist does when he prepares a shipment of flowers for sale, as described on page 20.

As soon as you bring your flowers home from the flower shop—or in from the garden—place them in the sink or in a bucket of cool water. Next, cut off 1 inch of stem, at a 45-degree angle, under water, to help the flowers rehydrate. If you don't already own a pair of florist's scissors, use a sharp kitchen knife, such as a paring knife, sharp household scissors, or cutting shears. Slicing the stems at a 45-degree angle exposes more of the pith under the skin of the stem to the water, plus it helps prevent air bubbles from entering the stem and blocking the absorption of water.

Flowers with fibrous or woody stalks or branches require more than a simple slice through the stem to allow them to absorb water. First of all, you'll probably have to use pruning shears to make your cuts, because

Quick tip

Some flowers need some special attention when you condition them.

- The stem ends of flowers such as daffodils and narcissus can be seared to seal them and help halt the excretion of toxic mucus. Water will then be absorbed through the sides of the stem. Poppy stems also need to be seared.
- To condition the thick, hollow stem of an amaryllis, tilt the stem up, fill it with water, then plug it with cotton so that water will not pour out when you transfer the cut flower to its container.

these branches are tough. (If the stem bears nodes, a good place to make a cut is right above a node.) After lopping off the end of the stem, slit it a couple of times with a sharp paring knife. Next, smash the slit end of the stem with a hammer to expose the pith to water. If you want to force buds, such as apple, cherry, or quince, to open more quickly, transfer the branches to warm rather than cool water after smashing their stems. The warmth should help speed up blooming.

After cutting, place your flowers in a vase or other container filled halfway with water and a packet of floral preservative. If you aren't going to arrange your flowers right away, leave them overnight in a cool place. A mudroom or sheltered porch is ideal, when outdoor temperatures allow. Otherwise, keep them in the kitchen (or where you plan to arrange them) but away from any source of heat or drafts. Most flowers can be massed together. A few types, however, make toxic pail-mates. Daffodils, for example, exude sticky mucus that's toxic to other flowers, so they should be conditioned separately. They should be allowed to rehydrate a bit longer, too.

water and floral food

Just like people, flowers need to be kept fed and comfortable. Flowers are a lot easier to satisfy than people, though. They're more like fish—all they need is clean water, plus a pinch of flower food. That's why florists always enclose a care-and-feeding tag with their floral displays. Basically, all you have to do is change out the water in your container on a regular basis—usually every couple of days. Supplementing the water with flower food not only helps nourish your blooms, it also helps the water stay clean longer. Available from your local florist or garden center, flower food—which florists call floral preservative—comes in packets and boxes. You simply measure out the dose indicated on the label.

Though convenient, you don't have to use store-bought floral preservative. It's easy to make your own. The healthiest solution includes three ingredients: something acidic to help flowers absorb water; something to fight bacteria; and a sugary substitute for the glucose the flower naturally manufactures when rooted in the soil. To create your own solution, stir 4 ounces of carbonated, nondietetic lemon-lime soda (which contains the sugar and minerals flowers crave) and 1 tablespoon of chlorine bleach into 1 gallon of water. Your flowers will love it!

Quick tip

Just as professional chefs allocate different knives to different tasks when they prepare a meal, it's a good idea for you to do the same with scissors. Typically, one pair of scissors is reserved for paper, another for ribbon, another for flowers, and so on. Over time, scissor blades, like the blade of a knife, grow dull. But, if you use craft scissors to cut paper, sewing scissors to cut ribbon, and florist's scissors to cut the stems of your flowers, all of your scissors should last longer.

setting up

Flowers always make people better, happier, and more helpful; they are sunshine, food, and medicine for the soul.

—Luther Burbank

Flower arranging is a lot like cooking, which is why we always give our Bloomnet® florists "recipes" for our projects. Our recipes include a list of "ingredients"—the flowers and foliage—used in the project, and in this book, we've provided a list of the tools you'll need as well. With a quick look at a recipe, you can shop for your ingredients and gather your tools in advance—just as a cook does when setting out to prepare a meal. We encourage you, though, to be creative with the recipes we've provided. Try out different flowers, if you like. Use a different container. Add decorative accessories, such as ribbon or faux fruit. Flower arranging is fun—so have fun with it! Here are some other basics that will help make working with flowers easy.

water

Whether a flower is rooted or cut, water is its best friend. Cut flowers last longer and look healthier if you keep them well-hydrated. As soon as you bring them home, you should immediately immerse their stems in a bucket or sink full of water. If your tap water is less than pure but still drinkable, you can add several drops of household bleach to the water to counteract the effects of any minerals or sediments that may be present in your water supply. Some people use bottled water (for their flowers), but that option, of course, is expensive.

When you're handling flowers, working near a sink is best, if possible. A sink with a tall, arched faucet is your best bet, if you have one, because it usually provides enough room underneath to tilt or stand most vases and containers when filling them with water. But not to worry, a watering can (and your bathtub) is a great substitute when you need to fill those tall vases or extra-large containers that won't fit in your kitchen sink.

The temperature of the water can also have an effect on flowers. Tepid water is usually best when you're storing flowers in their "holding pattern" before arranging them. Water that's too cold will shock the blooms; conversely, hot water may force them to open before you want them to. There are some instances when hot or warm water can work in your favor, though, too.

- If you want roses to unfurl immediately for a same-day arrangement, plunge their stems into hot water and they'll open right up.

- After cutting back hydrangea stems, thrust the flowers up to their heads in a pot of water you've brought just to a boil. After 30 seconds, transfer them to a pail of cold water, immersing them, once again, up to their heads. Drape dampened paper towels over the blossoms; let them rest at least 4 hours before arranging them.

- Plump up dehydrated roses by cutting back their stems an inch or so and immersing them in your bathtub in cool water. Allow the roses to hydrate about an hour. They should be revived and refreshed after their bath—just like you would be!

the work surface

Arranging flowers is much more comfortable when you can spread your flowers and tools over a broad and deep work surface you can walk around, such as a kitchen island or your kitchen table. An island or table allows you freedom of movement, so you can check out how your project is coming along, on all sides. If you don't have an island or table, a kitchen counter works just fine; you'll just need to turn your arrangement at various stages to see if you're filling it out evenly.

Quick tips

Sometimes even florists have to adapt their work areas. Here are a couple of hints to make flower arranging easier for you.

- If your kitchen table isn't quite the right height to work at, you can elevate your container by setting it on an overturned bucket or pail.

- Spreading plastic, such as a large, heavy-duty trash bag, over your work surface not only protects your surface—but it also makes cleanup a snap. Simply wrap everything up in the bag, and throw it away.

Arranging flowers can be messy. Most surfaces and tabletops are not stainproof. One way to protect yours is to cover it with a vinyl-coated tablecloth. (Vinyl-covered cloth can be found at any fabric store.) Another solution is newspapers. Many people swear by these. Newspapers are large enough to spread everything out on them, and, after you finish your arrangement, you can fold them over any debris and dispose of the paper and the mess, all in one fell swoop. Wet newsprint can stain a tabletop and your blooms, though, so try to change your newspapers as soon as they begin to look soggy.

Once you've decided where you want to arrange your flowers, it helps to organize how you want to work there. The easiest way to organize the area is to allocate one spot for your tools and another for laying out individual blooms when you're ready to add them to your arrangement. Set out one or two plastic cutting boards for messy tasks, such as smashing the ends of pithy stems or peeling off leaves. Plastic boards suit oozy jobs because they can be washed and "detoxed" in the dishwasher. And, keep a trash bucket handy for all those discarded stems and other debris that tend to pile up and clutter your work area.

tools and supplies

Florists store everything they need to create their arrangements in a place that's convenient to their work surface. If you can, why not set aside a drawer or cabinet for your own supplies? If you don't have enough space for this, you can keep your tools in a large canvas bag or tote. Garden centers carry a variety of bags and satchels—many have pockets—to organize your gear.

The basic florist's toolkit consists of just a handful of items: a sharp pair of florist's scissors, to cut stems of most flowers; a short-bladed florist's knife, to scrape off leaves and the bark from woody stems; pruning shears, to sever thick woody or fibrous stems; and wire cutters. You don't need to buy all of these supplies if you don't want to. You can substitute sharp household scissors for florist's scissors and a sharp paring knife for the florist's knife.

The toolkit is supplemented with florist's wire, which comes in several lengths and weights. Most wire is either 12 inches or 18 inches long. Heavy-gauge wire is most often used as a foundation for heavy arrangements such as garlands or swags; medium-gauge wire—the most-used type—is used to wrap and reinforce stems and to attach flowers and other plant matter to an arrangement; and fine-gauge wire is typically used to strengthen delicate blossoms or to "sew" flowers to an arrangement, such as a wreath. Medium- and fine-gauge wire are also used to wire fruit, when necessary.

Florists also rely on two different kinds of floral tape. Flexible green plastic floral tape, called stem wrap, may be paired with wire to bind and bundle several stems together, especially when creating bouquets and nosegays. Another type of floral tape looks like a green version of electrical tape; a darker green waterproof tape, it is often used to attach floral foam to a container, especially when the floral foam has to be saturated with water before beginning an arrangement.

Many arrangements are created using floral foam that's shaped like a brick. (The most common type of floral foam goes by the brand name OASIS®.) Floral foam is lightweight, rigid, and extremely dense, which makes it very easy to work with. All you have to do is gently insert stems into the foam, and they'll stay in place. You can also slice chunks off a brick to wedge in and around stems in elaborate arrangements. Floral foam is very easy to cut. A serrated knife works well for this purpose. To make things even easier, the brick is incised at the halfway mark, as well as into thirds. Our project recipes will give you the exact amounts you will need: ⅓, ½, or a full brick.

Quick tip

Floral foam comes in a variety of shapes and colors. Other versions include the ball, the cone, and the wreath. In our Chair Corsage project, we used a specialty version called an IGLU®, which is basically a cone enclosed in a plastic cage. In another project, our Birthday Flower Cake®, we used floral foam in a cake shape.

Traditionally, floral foam had been used in containers where it would not be seen, such as a basket. That's why it came in two basic colors, green and brown. (Brown is the color craftspeople specializing in dried flower arrangements prefer.) These days, you can find floral foam in a wider range of colors, so, if you want to use it in a clear vase, you can coordinate it with the color of your flowers or with the theme of your party.

Once cut, floral foam should be completely saturated with water before piercing it with a tool or a flower stem. To do this, simply drop the floral foam into a basin of water. As the water enters the foam, it will sink and bubbles will rise to the surface of the water. When bubbles no longer appear, that means the floral foam is fully saturated and ready to use in your arrangement.

Some of the projects on the pages that follow—such as garlands, swags, topiaries, and wreaths—require additional, specialized supplies. For example, florists often use a glue gun and glue sticks (or a glue pan and glue pellets) to fasten fresh flowers and floral decorations such as fake berries to their arrangements. Chicken wire may be used to create the horn-shaped base for a cornucopia. Fern pins help secure individual stems to floral foam in an arrangement.

working with a glue gun

Craftspeople and hobbyists such as woodworkers swear by glue guns because hot-gluing radically reduces the time and effort that goes into attaching one object to another. The tool's only shortcoming, paradoxically, is this very advantage: Hot glue hardens very quickly—in under a minute—which means there's no margin for error. Once the glue hardens, you can't fix a mistake. All that being said, a glue gun is a fabulous tool, especially for creating floral arrangements. Everything from buds and leaves to bark and moss can be hot-glued to a display.

Glue guns come in a variety of styles. All have a melting chamber (which holds the stick of glue), which is attached to a handle with a thumb-controlled grip that releases the glue, either in dabs or a steady stream. You can usually vary the heat of the glue—

from low for delicate materials (so you won't burn them) to high for sturdy ones. Glue sticks are purchased in packs; be sure to ask for florist's glue—as opposed to craft glue or woodworking glue.

- Keep glue sticks in the freezer: Heat and humidity can cause the glue to form "strings," which can clog the nozzle.
- Always keep the nozzle clean to prevent clogging.

The best glue guns have a "no-burn, drip-free" nozzle and an automatic shutoff or check valve to help prevent excess glue from drizzling from the nozzle. Some models come with multiple nozzles, so you can make dots or blobs or ribbons of glue, as the situation requires. Choose a model with a handle that feels comfortable in your hand and that has a grip you can manipulate easily with your thumb.

Handle glue guns with caution. Preheat the glue gun a full 10 minutes after turning it on, so that it can heat up properly. If you try to force the glue through before the melting chamber is hot, it can damage or break the glue feeder. Hot glue burns the skin, so keep a bowl of cold water nearby. In the event of a drip, plunge your hand in the water to cool and set the glue. Once set, you can pick the glue off your skin. Because of this hazard, you should never let children work with glue guns.

household aids

You may not need to purchase all of the supplies listed on the previous pages. In fact, you'll find many household supplies to complement your basic toolkit in your kitchen, laundry, home office, workbench, and sewing basket. Any sizeable bucket or pail, for example, will hold flowers in water. The large, handled buckets used for plaster and joint compound (found at paint stores and home centers) can stand in for a standard pail or bucket, or even a tall kitchen trash pail will do the job.

Here are some common household items you can use to help you create and maintain a flower arrangement.

Cardboard: Save the cardboards that professional launderers fold into clean shirts, as well as those that accompany mailings. You can cut cardboard into templates, such as for our Festive Party Placemats on page 75; you can also cut cardboard into "pads" to go under vases when you want to protect a tabletop or other surface. To make a pad, trace the base of your vase on the cardboard, and cut it out.

Claw hammer: Pound ends of woody or pithy stems to crush them.

Spray mister: Spritz and refresh blooms with a spray mister from the laundry room. (Don't use one that's been used for bleach or fabric softener, though!)

Straight pin: Use a straight pin (or needle) to prick the hollow stem right under a tulip blossom; this trick encourages water to be drawn up into the bloom.

Toothbrush: Use an old one to scrub the inside of a narrow-necked, scummy vase.

Turkey baster: Siphon off old water from—and add clean water to—an arrangement, without disturbing the flowers.

You might want to protect your clothing when arranging flowers. To do so, you can wear a large apron, preferably one with pockets—such as a barbecue apron—that can hold your scissors and other tools. Other options include an artist's smock or a large men's shirt with breast pockets. If your hands are susceptible to toxins, prickers, or thorns, lay in a supply of disposable, rubbery surgical or painter's gloves; these are flexible enough to allow you to manipulate your fingers with ease. Just be sure you don't grip stems with prickers or thorns too tightly; they may pierce the rubber.

FRESH thoughts®

Keep mason-style jars from tomato sauces, et cetera, to use as containers for quick, fun arrangements using bunches of flowers either from your garden or florist to give as pick-me-up or hostess gifts. It's easier for the recipient if the flowers are already in water—and the container is sweet to look at. Best of all, you've recycled it!

ribbons and decorative accessories

Many florists accent their arrangements with ribbon and other decorative accessories. You can, too! You probably already have a stash of ribbons on hand for birthday presents and other occasions, such as the holidays; why not keep some more on hand for flower arranging? Ribbons are made from many fabrics, such as organza, grosgrain, silk, satin, velveteen—and even paper. Wired ribbon is especially useful because it can be bent into—and will hold—a shape, indefinitely. As you expand your repertoire of floral arrangements, you may want to add a supply of tulle and cellophane to your flower-arranging drawer or tote. And, for fall and winter holidays, pick up some pinecones, fake berries, miniature gilt apples and pears, and preserved oak leaves. Craft and hobby shops (and garage sales and flea markets) are your best resource for many decorative items. Don't overlook the notions counter or home-sewing section at your local discount or department store—and your florist.

decorative accessories

Item	Use	Comments
ribbon	tie around bouquets; accent or tie up arrangement	comes in virtually unlimited range of widths, colors, and materials
cord	tie around bundles of flowers; tie up an arrangement	available in variety of thicknesses and colors
lace	tie around bouquets; accent arrangements	in strip form, available in variety of widths and colors
raffia	tie around bundles of flowers; accent arrangements	twist together strips to make thicker strip
cellophane	tie around a bouquet	may be clear or tinted
tissue	use with cellophane to wrap bouquets	comes in a wide range of colors; will wrinkle; water will cause it to fall apart
tulle or organza	wrap around stems	some is stiff; some, soft
miniature Styrofoam fruit; faux berries	once wired, attach to arrangements	often gold, to use in holiday decorations; berries are usually red
beads	string together to accent arrangements	available in wide range of sizes, shapes, and colors
pearl-headed pins	attach corsages; accent arrangements	pearls are just one type of pin; other colors available

Making a Floral Bow

Many bouquets and other flower arrangements are finished off with a floral bow. Everyone knows how to tie a basic two-loop bow, but we often attach special bows that have lots more loops, to enhance the overall effect of the displays. Sometimes we make bows with as many as 20 or 30 loops—or more! The trick is to make the loops in varying sizes so that they can fan out to form a perfect round shape. Usually, one roll of ribbon should contain enough yardage for a floral bow, but if you're making a particularly large one, buy an extra roll to be on the safe side. Using wired ribbon will ease the process. Here's how.

- To start your bow, make a small loop at one end of your ribbon, leaving the rest of the ribbon dangling free. Pinch the ribbon where the two parts of the ribbon meet; this spot indicates where the center of the bow will be.

- Pulling up the dangling ribbon, make a second loop the same size as the first, pinching it where its ends meet, as above, aligning them with the "center" of the bow made by the first loop.

- Continue making loops, making sure that every pair of loops is slightly larger than the pair before it. (If you run out of ribbon, you can always add new ribbon to a bow-in-progress by placing the end of the new ribbon at the center of the bow, where the loops meet—and continue to make loops from there.)

- When the bow achieves the fullness you like, take a 12-inch-long piece of fine-gauge florist's wire and wind two or three twists of the wire around the center of the bow, where all the loops meet, to secure it.

- Cut off the excess ribbon, then cut off the excess wire, except for 3 inches, so you can attach the bow to your arrangement. First, though, fan out the loops until the bow is round and full.

–Lisa Aliment
Redmond, WA

tools, equipment, and supplies

The chart below lists the various items you usually need to create a flower arrangement. As you'll note in the "Comments" column, you can substitute common household items for some of these tools. For example, you can often use household scissors instead of florist's scissors.

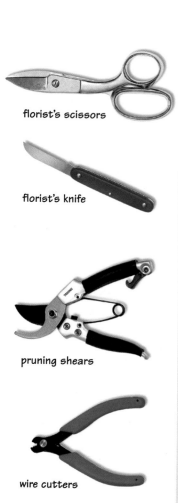

florist's scissors

florist's knife

pruning shears

wire cutters

basic florist's supplies

Item	Use	Comments
florist's scissors	cut most stems	have short, sharp, pointed blades; a pair of sharp household scissors works just as effectively
florist's knife	scrape, strip, or peel leaves off stems; strip bark off pith; cut stems	has a short, sharp blade; a sharp paring knife will serve the same purpose
pruning shears	cut thick, pithy, or woody stems	
florist's wire	use to reinforce stems, to attach flowers and leaves to an arrangement, or to act as a foundation for swags and garlands	comes in several gauges—heavy, medium, and fine; finest versions called spool wire or rose wire
wire cutters	snip and cut florist's wire	also good for cutting chicken wire

ITEM	USE	COMMENTS
floral foam	steady stems; hold them in position; when saturated with water, floral foam helps maintain constant moisture around stems	floral foam is very easy to work with; cuts easily, too; now available in colors besides green and brown
serrated knife	cut foam	a bread knife works well
glue gun and glue sticks; glue pan and glue pellets	hot-glue flowers, plant material, and decorative accessories to arrangement	faster and easier than attaching flowers or objects with wire
water tube or vial	hold blossom with extremely short stem; supply water to stem	cuplike, with pointed end to insert into arrangement; will give illusion of visually extending stems
floral stem wrap	wrap stems, individually, for strength, or when gathered in bunches	flexible and waterproof; green, to match most stems; also available in clear, white, and brown
fern pins	attach and secure stems to arrangement	may substitute hair pins—or cut and bend florists' wire for the purpose
waterproof florist's tape	attach floral foam to container; other, miscellaneous uses	not as flexible as stem wrap, reinforced with mesh

floral foam

colored floral foam

glue gun

glue sticks

glue pan

glue pellets

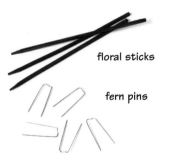

floral sticks

fern pins

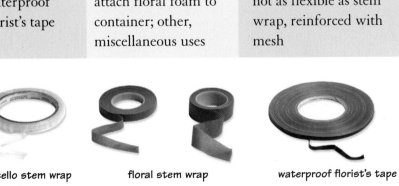

clear cello stem wrap   floral stem wrap   waterproof florist's tape

choosing a
container

*Arranging a bowl of flowers in the morning can give
a sense of quiet in a crowded day.*

—Anne Morrow Lindbergh

Mark Twain once said: "Clothes make the man." That's true of flowers, too. A flower arrangement is made by the vase or other container it "wears." The container you choose will make all the difference in how your arrangement will look.

Floral designers follow a number of guidelines when matching the shape of the arrangement to its container. Tall, spiky flowers tend to look their best in a tall cylindrical or rectangular container. By contrast, a wicker basket or lichen-covered flowerpot suits an informal tumble of roses accented with wildflowers such as Queen Anne's lace. Remember always that you can break the rules. For example, a tall container looks great showing off a tightly packed dome-shaped arrangement of flowers, such as peonies.

The main thing you have to figure out is the mood you want to convey. Do you want your arrangement to communicate a sense of formality and elegance, or do you want it to appear rustic and informal? Do you want to position every stem just so, so that the overall effect of the display is purposeful and deliberate? Or, do you want to mass your flowers so that they look as if they have been placed, just as you picked them, in your container?

glass and ceramic vases

Glass vases are a staple at most flower shops. Like a basic black dress that effortlessly allows a woman to look her best, a glass vase rarely distracts from the visual impact made by the flowers. In fact, glass enhances every type of flower, and it looks good in virtually any setting.

A glass vase may be clear, translucent, or frosted; it may be colored, patterned, or plain. A colored glass vase can also be translucent or frosted, or it may be so opaque you'd swear it was ceramic. To add texture, the glass manufacturer may cut or etch the surface of the vase in a geometric pattern or in a realistic one such as leaves.

Most vases conform to basic geometric shapes such as bubbles, cubes, cylinders, and rectangles, which florists know from experience will harmonize with every possible type of arrangement. The most popular shape of all is the ginger jar, followed by the bubble bowl (or fishbowl), which is especially pretty when it's used for centerpieces. Still others include the flared trumpet- or bell-shaped vase, the urn, and the so-called tazza, which resembles a stocky, wide-rimmed wine glass.

Unless they are specifically handcrafted as works of art, ceramic or glaze-coated pottery vases and containers tend to mimic their glass counterparts in size and shape. The primary reason for choosing a ceramic container is that it conceals less-than-attractive stems. A ceramic vase also provides a wonderful opportunity for the colors and patterns of your arrangement to play off against those in its setting.

nontraditional containers

Think outside the vase! Just because florists typically arrange their flowers in glass or ceramic vases, it doesn't mean you have to do the same. Open your drawers and look in your cupboards; you probably have all sorts of potential containers on hand. Once you've decided what might make a great container, it's easy to figure out

what flowers might suit it. For instance, a ceramic pie plate is the perfect shape and height for floating some pretty flower blossoms, such as anemones. An antique teacup makes a charming holder for a miniature nosegay of roses, say, or sweet peas. Other fun containers include eggcups, chunky china teapots, and mint julep cups, plus more tried-and-true choices, such as earthenware pitchers, enamel pitchers and bowls, crystal goblets, champagne flutes, and tumblers.

lining the container

A container does not have to be watertight. If it can't hold water, it can be made waterproof by inserting a plastic liner inside. Flower shops, nurseries, and garden centers carry an array of plastic liners in a variety of sizes and shapes, such as bowls and trays. If you don't want to bother with a commercial plastic liner, you can use any number of common kitchen items instead. A drinking glass, tumbler, or jar will hold flowers and water in virtually any upright container. A meat loaf pan is the perfect shape to insert in a window box. And don't overlook the plastic and aluminum foil containers that many convenience foods such as cook-and-serve dinners are packaged in. Take-out containers make good liners, too, even the lids. (For one fun "take-out" idea, see how we use Chinese food containers in our Good Fortune Bouquet™ project on page 233.)

If your container has an unusual shape, you can line it with a piece of heavy-duty plastic, such as a garbage bag. Measure and cut a piece of the bag to fit the container; position it inside, and attach and secure it at the rim of the container

containers in our Good Fortune Bouquet™ project on page 233.)

Quick tip

Floral designers sometimes use bubble wrap instead of floral foam when they want to secure flowers with short stems in an opaque container. All you need to do is cut a piece of bubble wrap to fit inside your container, pierce as many bubbles as blooms, and insert a flower stem into each hole.

FRESH thoughts®

As a container, a colander or salad strainer might put people off because of all those holes. No problem! Just drop a bowl into the colander or strainer, and you're all set.

with waterproof floral tape. Once you've completed your arrangement, tuck any exposed plastic under so it won't show. Finally, pack some sheet moss or reindeer moss around the base of the arrangement to hide the plastic.

Most containers are vulnerable to spills, especially if and when you change out the water, so you should always protect your tabletop or other surface with a moisture-resistant underlay. A saucer is the obvious solution. Cork cut to the dimensions of the base of a container is another option.

Any container has to be stable enough so that your flowers won't overpower it, so your vase (or any other container, for that matter) should feel solid and sturdy. Even if the sides of your vase are thin, the base should be weighty enough to support both the vase and your arrangement. You can add heft and stability to any vase with ballast. Two convenient forms of ballast are floral marbles or pebbles, both of which are sold at florists and garden centers. There are other, fun options, such as fruits like lemons and limes—they work well, plus they add visual interest. Another idea is to use sea glass.

making flowers behave

The size of the opening of the vase (or container)—and its shape—will affect how your flowers behave. The slightly flared sides of a trumpet-style vase, for example, allow flowers to relax as naturally in the vase as they would if held in your arms. The straight sides of a cylinder or tall rectangular vase, by contrast, hold stems erect.

Some vases are pinched in at the "waist," like an hourglass. This style works well when you want to highlight a large spray or two of a dramatic flower, such as gladiolus.

No matter what its style, a vase or container will be wide-mouthed, or it will have a narrow opening, like a bottle. The size of the opening obviously dictates how many flowers you'll be able to fit in the container. Florists often choose a container with a narrow neck when they want to show off one or two emphatic blooms, such as bird-of-paradise or calla lily.

Many floral arrangements require what florists term a "foundation," a stabilizing medium that they place at the bottom of a vase or container to hold stems upright and steady so they won't shift, droop, or fall. The most common type of foundation is floral foam. Another is the frog, a cagelike structure made of enameled wire, ceramic, or glass. Frogs are usually dome-shaped; some have porcupine-like "quills" that protrude from the surface to pierce stems. Since the invention of floral foam, frogs have passed out of favor, but you can find them at flea markets, or you can make one yourself by scrunching up some chicken wire into a ball.

bloomnet®
basics

Arranging flowers in a vase can be a little daunting when you first try it. Making a grid of clear or green waterproof florist's tape across the opening of the vase is a big help. Cut and crisscross four pieces of the tape across the opening of the vase, then place the flowers in the openings of the grid. Usually the largest flowers go in the center hole, to establish a focal point for the arrangement. The grid will keep your flowers in place and help prevent them from falling or tipping over the rim of the vase.

–Gayla Blackwell
Vine Grove, KY

arranging
flowers

The Amen of nature is always a flower.

—Oliver Wendell Holmes

Flowers make a great gift. No one can resist them! But, if you are planning to create your arrangements for a specific event instead, here are a few questions you might want to consider before you begin.

- What is the arrangement going to be used for? Is it going to commemorate a special occasion, such as a holiday or a birthday? Does the event have a theme, or is it going to be more informal and impromptu?

- What mood do you want your flower arrangement to convey? Do you want to evoke a romantic atmosphere, or do you want to make a dramatic statement? Do you want the arrangement to be formal and elegant—or rustic and carefree? Do you want it to echo a traditional design, or do you want it to look hip and up-to-the-minute?

- Finally, how and where is the arrangement going to be displayed? Is it going to be the focal point in the setting, or is it supposed to blend in with the background? Will you be able to walk all the way around it, or is it supposed to be viewed only from the front?

Florists usually follow certain specific design precepts when they create their arrangements, just as interior designers do. Typically, you should decide on colors and textures first, and then consider scale and balance.

Color and harmony: Choose flowers in a range of colors that complement or coordinate with the setting. If you want them to contrast with the setting, though, that's OK, too.

Texture: Choose flowers, leaves, and other plant material whose textures juxtapose nicely one with the other—and also complement the setting.

Scale: Choose flowers of a height and width that harmonize with other decorative elements in the setting. If you want to work with an overscaled arrangement, make sure it won't overwhelm the architecture in the setting. You don't want your arrangement to look like the Incredible Hulk!

Balance: Choose flowers and leaves that will not look top-heavy (or bottom-heavy) in the arrangement.

The overall dimensions of a floral arrangement tend to be dictated by the height of the tallest flowers. Florists usually start an arrangement by placing one or two of these at the center of the display, then build out from there. After positioning their focal blooms, they often rim the opening of the container with blossoms, then fill the gap between them with flowers and foliage until the arrangement has been completed to their satisfaction.

shaping the arrangement

Left to their own devices, cut flowers tilt, turn, curve, bend, and swoop in an exaggerated reenactment of how they grow in the wild. Even when you tame flowers to your will and design, some arrangements naturally take on the shape that more or less echoes the shape of the most assertive flower in the arrangement. A bouquet that consists primarily of hydrangea, for instance, will look round, and an arrangement bristling with tall flowers such as foxglove or gladioli will look spiky.

Experimenting with shapes is fun! One to try is the triangle. Simply slope your flowers from a tall bloom at the top to short-stemmed flowers at the rim of the container. One last thing to remember about shape is that flower arrangements—and their containers—tend to "shape" a particular mood, too. For example, a chunky cubic vase filled with nothing but tulips will look sleek and modernistic, while a bubble bowl brimming with peonies is the epitome of romance.

Quick tip

There are basically four styles of flower arrangements. They are:

casual	free-spirited/carefree
dramatic	bold/sultry
elegant	traditional/formal
romantic	old-fashioned/winsome

placing the arrangement

The most obvious locations for a floral display are a front-hall table, a coffee table, and the dinner table. Other pretty places to keep in mind are bedside tables, the floor, a stair landing, the rim of a bathtub that's set in a wide platform, a bookshelf, or a windowsill.

Each situation presents its own set of dictates. If you want to place your arrangement on a hall table with a mirror behind it, for example, don't forget to check the back of the display. The back should look almost as lush as the front—after all, it will be reflected in the mirror. By the same token, a centerpiece should look as lovely from above as it does on all sides, so your guests can admire it when they enter the dining room as well as when they are seated at the table. And, a bedside bouquet should be petite enough to share its table with a lamp and whatever else is at hand, such as an alarm clock, radio, or book.

spring

spring
thoughts

The calendar year may start on the first of January, but for anyone who loves flowers as much as we do, no year can officially begin until the first crocus pokes up through the melting snow. Then we know for sure that winter's monotones will soon be erased by spring rains and a fabulous rainbow of flowers. How wonderful it is to see the grass turn green once again—especially when it's carpeted with daffodils, jonquils, and tulips of every imaginable hue! We love to watch flowering trees and shrubs burst into bloom, too, because so many of them scent the air with delicious perfume. Think of apple and cherry blossoms. And lilac. And wisteria. Plus all the scented potted and cut flowers, such as hyacinth, freesia, and lily-of-the-valley, which you can pick up at your local flower shop.

As the season unfolds, days grow warmer and longer. At last, we get to wake up after the sun rises. We no longer have to go to and from work—or school—in the dark. Finally it's balmy enough to take a walk without having to bundle up in mittens and

mufflers. Gardeners can put away their snow blowers and replace them with lawn mowers and garden tools. And the soil is warm enough to plant all those seeds we ordered in the dead of winter.

Our springtime arrangements take their inspiration from the wonderful pastel colors and delicious scents of this miraculous season. Artichokes and asparagus and Easter eggs, for example, provide spontaneous and inventive containers for delicate blooms, such as tulips and alstroemeria. And, as a grand finale to the chapter, we offer a 1-800-FLOWERS® specialty—a Birthday Flower Cake® that's completely covered with flowers. Yes, it may be a birthday cake, but it can also celebrate any day you like, such as this season's Mother's Day—or any day of the year.

natural spring vase

One of the earliest harbingers of spring is asparagus. The first thing you'll notice is that these hardy perennials poke up—one by one—through a soft and frothy pale-green veil of fernlike foliage. As the weeks go by, the stalks thicken until they are strong enough to stand on their own.

What we love about asparagus is that we can whip up a few vases using this bamboolike veggie in a matter of minutes—even while waiting for the bunch used for a side dish to cook! Because of their natural rigidity, asparagus spears will stand tall around a drinking glass, tin can, or narrow, straight-sided glass jelly jar. All you need to keep them in line is the rubber band used to hold them together at the grocer's—plus ribbon, raffia, or twine to tie up the vase like a gift. Add the flowers of your choice, and you have a unique celebration of spring.

natural spring vase

astilbe

ruscus leaf

asparagus

alstroemeria

Level of Difficulty: Easy

Time: 15 minutes

Vase Life: Asparagus—3 to 5 days; flowers—7 to 10 days

FLOWERS AND VEGETABLES

1 bunch asparagus (approx. 20 spears), 4 stems alstroemeria, (approx. 16 blooms), 4 stems astilbe, 3 ruscus leaves

WHAT YOU NEED

- tall drinking glass (6 inches high, 2½ inches in diameter)
- sharp kitchen knife
- cutting board
- rubber band large enough to surround the glass; the thick band that secures the bunch of asparagus works perfectly
- 1 yard wired ribbon (we used 2-inch-wide pink organza ribbon)
- sharp craft or household scissors, for ribbon
- sharp florist's scissors, for flowers
- ¼ packet floral preservative

bloomnet®

basics

You can cover containers with a number of plant materials. Finish off your natural vases with a pretty ribbon. Here are two possibilities.

Sheet moss:

Cut enough sheet moss to cover the container. Using a glue gun, hot-glue the sheet moss to the container.

Lemon leaves:

Using a glue gun, attach lemon leaves (minus their stems) to the can with their tips pointing upward, so that they conceal the rim of the can. Repeat with a second layer of leaves, aligning the base of the leaves with the bottom of the can.

–Jay Casiano
New York, NY

1 Stand one asparagus spear against the glass and measure for the best height. You want the stalks to conceal the glass; their tips should extend a few inches above the rim of the glass—like a crown. Cut off the excess, straight across, at the base of the stalk.

2 Using the fresh-cut spear as a guide, lay out the asparagus on the cutting board and align the spears so that the tips are even. With the sharp knife, cut straight across the ends of all the stalks, making sure that their bases are flat so that the spears can stand upright.

3 Encircle the glass with the rubber band, placing it at the height you would like to tie your ribbon. Insert the asparagus spears between the rubber band and the glass, one by one, until the glass is concealed. The spears should abut each other and stand upright.

4 Using the wired ribbon, tie a big bow around the rubber band to hide it. With the craft or household scissors, snip the ribbon ends into V-shaped swallowtails.

Steps 1–2. Stand one asparagus spear against glass to establish best height; slice it–and ends of all spears–straight across. Set aside.

Step 3. Encircle glass with rubber band. Insert asparagus, spear by spear, between the band and glass, until glass is concealed.

Steps 4–7. Tie ribbon around rubber band. Cut and condition flowers; arrange in glass filled one-third with water and floral food.

5 Cut and condition all the flowers, making sure some are taller than others; all of their stems should be longer than the asparagus spears.

6 Fill the glass one-third full with water and stir in the floral preservative.

7 Arrange the alstroemeria first, then add the astilbe to fill out the arrangement. Insert the ruscus leaves, as desired.

Quick tip

If you are going to display your asparagus vase on a tablecloth or runner, place it on a small plate, to protect the fabric from moisture or stains. Place an ice cube on the plate daily. As ice melts, the cold water will keep your asparagus fresh longer.

nature's place card

Like asparagus, artichokes are harvested in the spring. Artichokes are remarkably versatile: You can turn them into votive holders or, as here, into combination mini-vases and place card holders to decorate a table for a festive springtime lunch or dinner. This fanciful place card is a great way to bring the garden indoors, too, and, again, takes only minutes to create—including writing names on the cards.

Even though you can slice into almost any small, firm, and thick-skinned vegetable to create a natural vase and name-card holder for a table setting, an artichoke is the most convenient because its rigid petals are readymade to grasp a small card. The tips of the petals end in sharp prickers, though, so you may want to snip these off if you are hosting a party where children will be present. To turn your holder into a miniature vase, as pictured here, all you need to do is push aside the top petals and scoop out the core (and heart) of the vegetable, to make room for your flowers. We used a grapefruit spoon for this because it has a serrated edge. Repeat the process for as many artichokes as you'll need for your party. And there you are!

nature's place card

tulip

caspia

artichoke

Level of Difficulty: Easy

Time: per artichoke: 15 minutes

Vase Life: 3 days

FLOWERS AND VEGETABLES

1 artichoke, 6 tulips, 1 stem caspia

WHAT YOU NEED

- sharp paring knife

- grapefruit spoon

- shot glass or narrow votive holder

- sharp florist's scissors, for tulips

- place card

- pen or marker

bloomnet®
basics

If you don't have shot glasses or glass votives on hand, you can use wet floral foam to hold flowers in the artichoke. Cut a piece of floral foam that's large enough to fit the artichoke cavity; saturate it thoroughly with water, and stuff it into the cavity.

–Joanna Zeruos
Bethel Park, PA

1 With your finger, separate the topmost petals of the artichoke to open the center cavity over the heart of the vegetable.

2 Using the paring knife, cut into the core of the artichoke to loosen the flesh.

3 With the grapefruit spoon, scoop out the flesh and heart; discard them both.

4 Insert the shot glass or votive holder into the cavity of the artichoke and fill the shot glass with water.

5 Cut the tulip stems with the florist's scissors so that the flowers will poke up above the top of the artichoke. Arrange the flowers in the shot glass. Accent them with sprigs snipped from the stem of caspia.

6 Write out place cards. Insert each one behind a leaf of each artichoke. Place artichokes on individual plates.

Steps 1–4. Push apart top leaves of artichoke and remove center and heart. Insert votive holder in cavity.

Steps 4–5. Fill votive holder with water. Snip tulips to height of holder and arrange as desired, preferably so they lean over rim.

Step 6. Insert each place card behind a leaf of each artichoke.

Quick tip

Tulips are special, not only because they come in every color and color combination imaginable, but also because they keep on growing, even after they're picked! So, you can cut them a bit short—and they'll make up the difference in no time.

easter
eggcups

Dying eggs is a tradition that hearkens back to pagan times when eggs were boiled with flower petals to color them, then exchanged as gifts to celebrate the rebirth of spring. Dyed eggs' colorful hues and simple beauty remind all of us—kids and adults alike—of the good things this fresh new season has in store. So, what better partner is there for dyed eggs than spring's other favorite—flowers!

One way we love to use dyed eggshells is to convert them into unique mini-vases for spring blooms. To do so, blow the egg out of its shell, then color the shell. Once the dye has set, snip out an opening at the top of the shell, and fill it with whatever flowers tickle your fancy. The kinds of flowers that look best are ones with small heads and narrow stems, like alstroemeria, miniature daffodils (also called Daffodils 'Tete-a-Tete'), small tulips, waxflower, or monte casino. This project is so easy even the kids can help—as long as you promise them you'll boil some additional eggs they can color separately for their Easter egg hunt!

easter eggcups

miniature daffodils

alstroemeria

Level of Difficulty: Easy

Time: After dying eggs, about 10 minutes

Vase Life: 1 week

FLOWERS AND EGGS

1 egg per eggcup, 1 stem alstroemeria or
3 daffodils 'Tete-a-Tete' (miniature daffodils)

WHAT YOU NEED

■ 1 pushpin

■ 1 12-inch-long piece of medium-gauge florist's wire
   (you can use the same piece of wire for all eggs)

■ small kitchen bowls, to hold eggs as they are dyed

■ egg dying kit

■ embroidery or nail scissors

■ eggcups, one for each egg

■ sharp florist's scissors

Quick tip

Because dyed eggs are so
colorful, you can mix up
all sorts of flowers that
bear small to medium
blooms in a variety of
hues. Here are a few
other options for flowers
that would work well in
eggcups:

monte
casino

tulip

rose

waxflower

1 Using the pushpin, pierce each end of a raw egg.

2 Insert the medium-gauge wire through the holes in the egg made by the pushpin. The wire will break the yoke, making it much easier to blow out the egg. Blow out the egg white and yolk into a bowl.

3 Prepare the egg dyes in individual bowls according to package instructions. Immerse an egg in each bowl of dye. Remove the egg from the dye when it achieves the desired color. Allow it to dry. (You may need to dip the egg in and out of the dye from time to time to distribute color evenly over the surface of the egg.)

4 Using the embroidery or nail scissors, snip away at the hole at the top of the eggshell until it is the size you want. Rinse out the eggshell and place it in an eggcup. Fill the eggshell with water. Repeat for all the eggs. **Note**: Water may leak out of the bottom hole in the eggshell, but this won't matter because the eggcup functions like a mini-reservoir, to hold excess water.

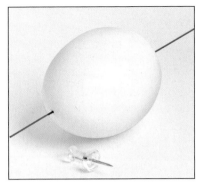

Steps 1–2. Pierce both ends of egg with pushpin; push piece of wire through to puncture yolk. Blow out egg.

Steps 3–4. Prepare dyes according to package directions. Immerse each egg until it achieves color desired. Snip opening in small end of egg.

Step 5. Cut flowers off stems to a length that will fit the eggshells. Pour water in each shell; arrange flowers in eggs.

5 Cut the stems of the flowers to a length that will fit the eggshells. Arrange the flowers, as desired, in the eggshells.

FRESH thoughts®

Easter Eggcups make wonderful place cards at springtime table settings, especially at a festive holiday brunch. Using acrylic or metallic craft paint or a marker, write the name of your guest on the eggshell—or on the eggcup. After your meal is over, give your guests their eggcup place cards to take away as favors. Another idea is to scatter the eggcups over the entire table. The more eggcups you display on the tabletop, the more abundant and farm-fresh your table will look.

festive
party
placemat

Special occasions bring out the best in all of us—don't you agree? If you have a particular event coming up, be it a birthday, or Mother's Day, or a graduation, now's the time to go all out to make the dining room look as inviting as possible—especially the table. A tabletop offers so many opportunities to decorate with flowers, from the centerpiece to napkin holders.

One wonderful way to set off your linens and dinnerware is with a placemat made from leaves and flowers. Your guests will think they are dining in a meadow! A floral placemat can be down-to-earth, featuring a simple bed of lemon leaves or magnolia leaves or sheet moss, or it may mix together a colorful variety of blossoms and buds—plus leaves. If you select flowers that can be air-dried, you will be able to preserve your placemats so they can be used and enjoyed again and again.

festive party placemat

lemon leaves

heather

seeded eucalyptus

statice

hypericum berries

caspia

Level of Difficulty: Easy

Time: ½ hour per placemat

Vase Life: Fresh, 3-5 days if refrigerated when not in use
  Dry, a few weeks

FLOWERS AND LEAVES

4 or 5 stems lemon leaves (approx. 65–70 leaves),
2 stems heather, 2 stems statice, 1 stem caspia,
1 stem seeded eucalyptus, 2 stems hypericum berries

WHAT YOU NEED

■ 1 10- or 10½-inch-diameter dinner plate

■ pencil or marker

■ cardboard, slightly larger than dinner plate you are using;
be sure you have enough cardboard to accommodate the
number of placemats you need for your party

■ sharp craft or household scissors, for cardboard

■ glue pan and glue sticks, or glue gun and glue sticks;
we used a glue pan because it is so much quicker!

■ sharp florist's scissors, for flowers and leaves

bloomnet®
basics

Hot glue will blacken the
bottoms of the lemon
leaves, so make sure each
leaf you add to the placemat covers the bottom of
the leaf beneath it.

Also: If you find that
you are getting strings of
glue on your placemat,
never fear! Simply sweep
a hair dryer set on low
over the project and the
glue strings will disappear!

—Carol Rose
Rapid City, SD

1 Using the dinner plate as a template, draw a circle on the cardboard. Cut out the circle and set aside.

2 Cut the lemon leaf at the base of the leaf where it meets the stem; cut off nub at base of leaf so that the leaf will lie flat (see photo). Repeat for all lemon leaves.

3 With florist's scissors, snip the sprigs of heather, statice, caspia, seeded eucalyptus, and hypericum berries to 2- to 3-inch lengths; set aside.

4 Melt the glue in the glue pan; dip the bottom of the lemon leaf in the hot glue; press the leaf into place at the rim of the cardboard circle. Repeat process until the cardboard is encircled by leaves.

5 Dip a sprig of heather—or of any flower—in the glue pan and glue it to the cardboard so that it overlaps a lemon leaf. Repeat with the rest of the sprigs, mixing them as desired, until you have created a ring of flowers. Make sure you leave the tips of the lemon leaves exposed.

Steps 2–3. Cut stems of flowers to 3-inch lengths. Cut off nub of lemon leaves at the base.

Step 4. Press leaf into place at rim of cardboard circle.

Step 5. Glue a smaller ring of flowers to the cardboard.

Step 6. Repeat step 4 until cardboard is covered.

6 Repeat Step 4 until the cardboard is completely covered with lemon leaves.

FRESH thoughts®

Preserving and Storing Your Floral Placemats

When properly stored, your placemat should last for several weeks. You should be able to use it four times at least—if not more. After your party is over, gently wrap each placemat in tissue, leaving plenty of room around each flower to prevent crushing. Place tissue-wrapped placemats in a plastic grocery bag and store in the fridge until you need it again.

chair
corsage

Many people envision a corsage as the gift a boy brings to his date on the night of a prom. At many of the weddings we have worked on, we tie corsages on the chairs that will be occupied by the bride and groom—to mark their places of honor. But there's no reason why a corsage can't be made for other occasions as well. The corsages featured here, for example, are worn by all the chairs in this dining room, to complement our Festive Party Placemats (and Citrus Flowerpots on page 83) at a once-in-a-lifetime birthday brunch.

Placing flowers in unexpected spots livens up a room in no time, and decorating your guests' chairs tells them that they are special, too. Let them take their corsages home afterward, along with your recipes for favorite dishes you made for the meal. That way they will remember your hospitality forever!

chair corsage

Level of Difficulty: Moderate
Time: ½ hour per corsage
Vase Life: 2–3 days

FLOWERS AND LEAVES

1 stem Asiatic lilies (3 flowers), 2 roses, 4 stems heather, 2 stems solidago, 1 stem waxflowers, 1 stem seeded eucalyptus

WHAT YOU NEED

- 1 floral-foam IGLU® (a 2⅝ by 2½-inch cone-shaped piece of floral foam caged in plastic)

- 2 24-inch-long pieces of ribbon, of your choice

- sharp florist's scissors

Quick tip

When creating an arrangement that requires flowers of different sizes and stems of different lengths, it's best to eyeball each flower against the arrangement before cutting its stem.

bloomnet®
basics

If you can't find a floral-foam IGLU® at your florist or craft shop, you can make your own with floral foam and chicken wire. With a serrated knife, cut one-third brick of floral foam into a dome shape. Using wire cutters, cut a piece of chicken wire large enough to completely encase the floral-foam dome; wrap it around the form, inserting the exposed ends into the floral foam.

–Lance Williams
Los Angeles, CA

1 Soak the floral-foam IGLU® in water.

2 Loop the ribbons through opposite sides of the cage that encases the floral-foam IGLU®.

Step 2. Pull pre-cut ribbons through opposite sides of floral-foam cage.

3 Lay the IGLU® flat on your work surface, with the ribbons pulled out of the way. Cut and position the largest focal flower—here, one of the Asiatic lilies—on top of the IGLU®, taking care not to stain your fingers with the powdery coating on their stamens. Add the other two lilies, wherever desired.

4 Cut the roses to 3-inch lengths and insert them into the IGLU®, making sure they tuck in close to the lilies.

Steps 3–4. Cut and position one Asiatic lily on top of IGLU®; cut and add two more lilies and two roses, massing them around the first lily.

5 Cut the stems of heather, solidago, waxflowers, and seeded eucalyptus into sprigs. As you cut off each sprig, insert it into a gap in the arrangement. Mix up the sprigs as you go, inserting them, one by one, until you achieve the fullness desired for your corsage.

6 Tie the completed corsage to the back of the chair with the ribbons.

Step 5. Snip and add sprigs of remaining flowers, inserting each sprig in a gap and filling out corsage to desired fullness.

citrus flowerpots

A visit to any florist or garden center will turn up stacks and stacks of flowerpots made from the rosy clay called terra-cotta. For centuries, terra-cotta has been the material of choice for potting and showcasing plants because it retains water and "breathes" at the same time. For this reason, you'll want to line your flowerpots so they won't leak onto the surface of your table.

Like cornucopias, flowerpots filled with flowers and fruit imply profusion and plenty. As a natural way to decorate any tabletop, Citrus Flowerpots—or plain floral ones—can't be beat. Cluster lots of pots of different sizes on your table, and you'll signal to one and all that you have a generous, openhearted spirit, just like Mother Nature. Here, we show you how to decorate the medium-size flowerpot in our photo; you'll see that all of the pots incorporate all the elements listed—but in different quantities and configurations. It's up to you how you want to make yours. Like we always say: Just have fun with it!®

You may find that new flowerpots look too antiseptic and unnatural. Giving them a rusticated patina is easy (see how on page 85).

citrus flowerpots

Level of Difficulty: Moderate

Time: 2 hours, including paint-drying time, per flowerpot

Vase Life: 1 week; the pots, of course, can be used over and over

FLOWERS AND FRUITS

1 stem seeded eucalyptus, 1 lemon, 1 lime, 3 strawberries, 2 sunflowers, 2 roses, 1 stem alstroemeria (approx. 5 blossoms), 1 stem sprengeri (commonly known as asparagus fern), 1 stem solidago, 1 stem caspia

WHAT YOU NEED

- newspapers or other protective material, to protect work surface from paint
- 1 6-inch-tall terra-cotta flowerpot
- 1 can white spray paint, available from the art store
- natural sea sponge
- 1 pint sage-green latex paint, from the art store
- bucket large enough to submerge flowerpot in
- plastic painters' or surgical gloves, or rubber gloves
- 1 can gold spray paint, from the art store
- clear plastic liner
- ½ brick floral foam
- green waterproof florist's tape
- sharp craft or household scissors, for tape
- 2 6-inch-long florist's sticks
- 1 9-inch-tall, 3-inch-wide pillar-style candle
- sharp florist's scissors, for flowers
- 10 12-inch-long pieces of medium-gauge florist's wire

bloomnet®
basics

You can "age" a terra-cotta flowerpot by encouraging mildew to grow on its surface. As a first step, thoroughly douse the flowerpot with water. Next, encase it in plastic wrap, to keep it damp. Within a couple of days, mildew should begin to appear. When the pot starts to dry out, spritz the surface with water; repeat the process until the flowerpot accumulates the amount of mildew for the look you want. You can then spray it with hairspray or artist's fixative to "set" the mildew.

–Georgeanna Spinello
Murrysville, PA

1 Lay out newspapers over your work surface. Spray-paint the flowerpot white, inside and out, and allow it to dry, bottom side up.

2 Using the sponge, dab the outside of the flowerpot in a random pattern with the green paint. Allow it to dry.

3 Fill the bucket with water. Wearing rubber gloves, spray a film of gold paint onto the surface of the water.

4 Dip the flowerpot into the water, in a quick in-out swirling motion, to pick up the gold specks. Allow it to dry.

5 Place the plastic liner in the flowerpot. Stuff the floral foam into the pot, with the top higher than the rim.

6 Using the florist's tape, attach the two florist's sticks, one on either side of the candle. Center the candle on top of the floral foam. Insert the sticks into the floral foam to secure the candle.

7 Cut the stems of seeded eucalyptus to 3-inch sprigs and insert the sprigs into the floral foam around the rim of the flowerpot.

Steps 1–2. Paint entire pot with white paint. When dry, sponge on green paint in random pattern.

Step 3. Fill bucket with water; spray gold paint over surface of water.

Step 4. Swirl flowerpot in gold-flecked water, in quick in/out motion, to pick up gold flecks.

Steps 5–6. Place plastic liner in pot, then floral foam to fit. Attach floral sticks to pillar candle with tape; press fortified candle partway into foam.

8 Wire the lemon, the lime, and each strawberry (see Wiring Fruit on page 196).

9 Insert the twisted wires that secure the fruit into the floral foam, positioning the fruit as desired.

10 Cut the stems of the rest of the flowers to 3-inch lengths, and insert them one by one as desired, to fill out the arrangement.

Steps 7–8. Cut flowers and floral sprigs to 3-inch lengths, then wire fruit; twist wires together.

Steps 9–10. Insert wired fruit in floral foam, where desired. Add flowers and sprigs, where desired, around pot rim until candle is surrounded.

flower topiary

Topiaries date back to ancient Egypt, when rows of date palms were force-cut into the shapes of cones. In later practice throughout Europe, topiaries were carved from hedges, bushes, and shrubs that were trimmed into fanciful shapes for the amusement of passersby. Shapes ran the gamut from cones, balls, and poodle-cut pom-poms to animals as winsome as dogs, giraffes, and elephants. Today's topiaries are not restricted to formal landscaping schemes. Many varieties are potted: Some are crafted from live herbs, such as rosemary, or from tamed greens, such as boxwood.

Creating a topiary no longer requires that you adhere to Nature's timetable. You can make a topiary for yourself—or for a friend—in under an hour! All you need are floral foam and the greens and flowers of your choice, as well as a dowel and flowerpot to act as the support and showcase for your desired shape. We chose flowers that air-dry well so that our topiary would last even longer than the two weeks we've indicated. Boxwood begins to wrinkle a bit after the first week, but we can live with that.

flower topiary

waxflower

baby's breath

boxwood

short-stem rose

delphinium

Level of Difficulty: Moderate
Time: 1 hour
Vase Life: 1 to 2 weeks

FLOWERS, GREENS, AND SHEET MOSS

1 6 x 6-inch piece sheet moss, approx. ⅓ pound boxwood, 12 short-stem roses, 2 stems baby's breath, 3 stems delphinium, 2 stems waxflowers

WHAT YOU NEED

- newspaper, to protect work surface
- 1 can gold spray paint, available at an art supply store
- 1 5-inch-high, 6-inch-diameter terra-cotta flowerpot
- 1 24-inch-long, ¾-inch-diameter wooden dowel
- 1 2- by 2-inch piece of duct tape, if necessary
- screwdriver
- 2 2-inch-long screws
- 1 brick floral foam, cut in half
- plaster of Paris
- large bowl or small pail, to mix plaster of Paris in
- sharp florist's scissors

Quick tip

It doesn't have to be springtime to make a topiary. For a summertime topiary, you can add seashells to the base to bring the ocean breezes inside!

Topiaries make great Christmas gifts, too. All you have to do is dot the boxwood with miniature red roses or other red flowers of your choice to suit the season.

1 Lay out the newspaper on your work surface. Spray-paint the outside of the flowerpot and the wooden dowel with gold spray paint. Allow to dry. Place duct tape over the hole on the inside of the flowerpot, if it has one.

2 With a screwdriver, screw one screw into the dowel, about 2 inches from one end. Push one chunk of floral foam about 3 to 4 inches down the opposite end of the dowel.

3 Screw the second screw about 3 inches from the end at the opposite end of the dowel (or an inch or so from the chunk of floral foam).

4 Mix a small batch of plaster of Paris in the bowl (enough to fill the flowerpot one-third full), following package instructions. As quickly as possible, pour the wet plaster into the flowerpot, covering the duct tape. Insert the dowel (including the first screw) into the plaster of Paris until the dowel hits the bottom of the flowerpot.

5 Push the chunk of floral foam down the dowel, pressing until the floral foam can be pushed partway into

Step 1. Spray outside of flowerpot and dowel with gold spray paint.

Steps 2–3. Insert one screw in dowel, 2 inches from end. Push one chunk of floral foam down dowel to rest against screw. Screw second screw into opposite end of dowel.

Steps 5–8. Push dowel into plaster until dowel rests on bottom of pot. Push second chunk of foam onto other end of dowel until it rests against screw. Cover floral foam in pot with sheet moss. Snip and add boxwood to top chunk of foam.

Step 9. Cut flowers to 2-inch lengths and insert in boxwood ball, as desired, to complete topiary.

the wet plaster. Allow the plaster to set around the foam and dowel, about 20 minutes.

6 Cover the floral foam (and the gap between it and the sides of the flowerpot) with sheet moss, so that the moss mounds slightly above the rim of the flowerpot.

7 Push the second chunk of floral foam onto the dowel until it rests against the top screw.

8 With your hands or florist's scissors, break or snip off sprigs of the boxwood and insert them, sprig by sprig, into the floral foam at the top of the dowel, turning the flowerpot as you work until the topiary assumes a pretty, round shape.

9 With florist's scissors, cut the roses back to 2-inch lengths. Insert them in the boxwood (and into the sheet moss), as desired. Repeat the process, cutting sprigs of baby's breath, delphinium, and waxflower, mixing them and inserting them where desired.

birthday
flower cake®

Of all the designs we have come up with over the years, our Birthday Flower Cake® wins hands down as the most loved—and most appreciated—by everyone who receives one as a gift. In fact, in return, we've collected literally thousands of letters and thank-you notes telling us how much fun it is to receive one of these cakes. Now, we're excited and happy to share with you our secret about how to make this beautiful creation. Consider it a gift from us.

Not only is our Birthday Flower Cake® sinfully easy to do your-self, but it's also sinfully easy for any calorie-counter to resist—eating, that is! Otherwise, it's absolutely irresistible. All you need is a cake-shaped floral-foam foundation and lots and lots of your favorite flower, and you're all set. We've chosen cushion poms and mini-carnations because they are sturdy, and they have lush, full heads with petals that won't fall off. Just remember, our Birthday Flower Cake® is to be admired only—not eaten. For that kind of a treat you still have to go to the bakery!

birthday flower cake®

rose

cushion pom

mini-carnation

Level of Difficulty: Moderate
Time: 45 minutes
Vase Life: 1 week or more

FLOWERS

40 cushion poms, 16 mini-carnations, 1 rose

WHAT YOU NEED

- glue gun and glue stick
- 1 6-inch-diameter cake-shaped block of floral foam
- 1 6-inch-diameter plastic saucer with a slightly flared rim, available at your florist's
- 6 fern pins
- 1 yard organza-and-tulle doily trim, available at a craft-supply store
- sharp craft or household scissors, for doily trim and ribbon
- sharp florist's scissors
- 6 birthday candles
- 3 yards ½-inch-wide satin ribbon
- straight pins

bloomnet®
basics

Our cake happens to be round, but you can also make a tiered cake by cutting bricks of floral foam in two or three different sizes and hot-gluing them together so they stack. For extra reinforcement, insert one or two floral sticks through the stack.

A square or cube-shaped cake looks nice, too, or, if you are really pressed for time, you can even make a single slice.

–Kevin King
Fort Myers, FL

1 Hot-glue the cake-shaped floral foam to the plastic saucer and allow the glue to set.

2 Immerse the plate and floral foam in water until the foam is completely saturated.

3 Using the fern pins, attach the doily trim around the base of the foam, making sure it covers the rim of the saucer. Cut off the excess with craft scissors.

4 With florist's scissors, cut the cushion poms off their long stems, leaving a 2-inch stem on each pom. Insert the poms around the base of the floral foam, one by one, so they slightly overlap the doily trim. Add a second tier of poms above the first, aligning blossoms with those in the first tier. Repeat the process for a tier of mini-carnations.

5 Insert a final circle of cushion poms on top of the cake, making sure all are level. Insert the rose at the center of the cake. Insert the birthday candles between the mini-carnations and cushion poms on top of the cake.

Steps 1–3. Hot-glue floral-foam "cake" to plastic plate; saturate foam in water. Attach doily trim to "cake" base with fern pins.

Step 4. Cut cushion poms to 2-inch lengths. Insert row of poms above doily trim; add second tier of poms above first.

Step 4 (continued). Add tier of mini-carnations, angling stems to secure them to floral foam.

Step 5. Add final circle of cushion poms; insert a single rose at center of top of "cake."

6 Cut and tie the ribbon into little bows and attach the bows with straight pins right below the mini-carnations. Measure, cut, and add swags of ribbon, if desired, securing their ends behind the loops of the bows with straight pins.

Quick tip

Cake-shaped floral foam can be found at florists' shops, but if you have trouble finding one for your project, you can carve a cake shape out of a brick of floral foam using a serrated knife.

Step 6. Make ribbon bows; pin to cake below mini-carnations, where desired, with straight pins. Add swags of ribbon, if desired, between bows.

spring table

One of the purest delights of spring is watching brown, dried-out lawns and fields turn green and lush—even if it means getting the mower out of the back of the garage or toolshed! So for this project we took our cue from Mother Nature with little "yards" of wheatgrass. The look and feel of fresh grass is perfect for a fun, spring centerpiece.

The bright green sets off the pretty colors of the flowers, and it looks wonderfully healthy and abundant, too. We also combined old and new by decorating the rest of the accessories with a striped grosgrain ribbon, giving the table setting a vintage and trendy look at the same time. We used flowers that matched the colors of our ribbon. You can coordinate with flowers that match, contrast, or whatever makes you feel like spring is here!

spring table

wheatgrass

pink hyacinth

purple-blue hyacinth

Level of Difficulty: Easy
Time: 1 hour for all pieces
Vase Life: 1-2 weeks

FLOWERS AND GRASS

1 flat of wheatgrass, 14 purple-blue hyacinths, 20 pink hyacinths

WHAT YOU NEED

- high-gloss white spray paint
- 9½-inch-long by 8-inch-deep by 2-inch-high wooden box, available from an art or craft store
- heavy-duty black plastic bag
- sharp household scissors, for plastic and ribbon
- sharp paring knife
- 48-inch-long piece of 1½-inch-wide blue-striped grosgrain ribbon
- fabric glue, available from a craft store
- 2 6-inch-high by 3⅓-inch-diameter cylindrical glass vases
- sharp florist's scissors
- waterproof green floral tape
- 74-inch-long piece of ⅞-inch-wide pink-striped grosgrain ribbon
- 2 pearl-headed pins, available from a florist or craft shop
- packet of floral preservative
- 10 small D rings, available from a craft or fabric shop

bloomnet®
basics

Wheatgrass is typically sold in 10- by 20-inch flats. You can slice off smaller sections with a sharp paring knife. The rest of the grass need not go to waste. Place tufts in little glasses at each place setting or in mint julep cups. To maintain wheatgrass, spritz it with water every couple of days and add water daily. You can trim it, too, using sharp scissors. Wheatgrass should last up to two weeks.

–C. Brent Conatser
Nashville, TN

1 With the spray paint, spray the wooden box inside and out; allow to dry. Cut a piece of black plastic bag to fit and lay it in the box so that it covers sides as well.

2 With the paring knife, cut an 8-inch by 9$\frac{1}{2}$-inch mat of wheatgrass, set aside.

3 With the scissors, cut the blue-striped ribbon into four 12-inch strips. Using fabric glue, glue the strips of ribbon around the top and bottom of each of the two vases.

4 Gather 7 purple-blue hyacinths in one hand; surround them with 10 pink hyacinths. Cut off all stems straight across to 6-inch lengths. Secure the stems with floral tape. Repeat the process for the second bouquet.

5 Cut two 6-inch strips from the piece of pink-striped ribbon. Wrap one strip around each bouquet, covering the floral tape, securing each with a pearl-headed pin.

6 Fill each vase with water and floral preservative to just below the bottom-ribbon line; place the bouquets in the vases, and fluff their blooms.

Step 1. Spray-paint wooden box white. Once dry, line with black plastic, cut to fit.

Step 3. Cut four strips of blue-striped ribbon, to go around two cylindrical vases. Glue strips to top and bottom of each vase.

Step 4. Gather blue hyacinths, with pink ones around them; cut stems straight across to 6-inch lengths; wrap with floral tape.

Step 6. Place bouquets in vases filled to height of bottom ribbon with water.

To make "belts":

1 Cut one 38-inch strip and four 9-inch strips from the remainder of the pink ribbon.

2 Thread the long strip of ribbon through one D ring; fold $\frac{1}{2}$ inch of ribbon at one end over the ring, to make a hem, and glue it to the back of the ribbon strip. Repeat the process at the other end of the ribbon with the second D ring—but fold the $\frac{1}{2}$-inch hem in the opposite direction around the ring. (When you join the two D-rings, both hems will then be on the inside.) Wrap and belt the box. Place the wheatgrass in the finished, plastic-lined box.

3 Repeat Step 2 for all four napkin belts. Roll up each napkin, belt it, and slip a sprig of hyacinth under each belt.

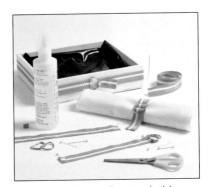

Steps 1–3. Cut pink-striped ribbons for box and napkin rings. Fold hems over D rings, one by one, gluing each to secure. Belt box and rolled-up napkins.

out of the garden

"April showers bring May flowers." So the saying goes—but what about March or even the end of February? What about all those days and weeks when you know the earth is unbuckling from winter's icy grip? And what about all those rainy days that force you to stay indoors?

Just as nurseries and greenhouses nudge their seedlings and force bulbs so people can enjoy their often-scented flowers when it's still cold outside, we, too, love to get a head start on spring by forcing bulbs of our own (see Forcing Bulbs on page 102) and by "planting" little indoor gardens all over the house. So, even if you don't have a real garden of your own outside, you can always create a miniature one inside. Indoor blooming gardens inject doses of vibrant color into any room. "Come on, Mother Nature—wake up!" they seem to say. "Come on! Warm up! Let's go!"

For this indoor garden, we used a pretty hat box (but any box, bowl, or planter would do) and filled it with miniature roses, daisies, and ivy. If your box is large enough to place all your pots inside, you don't even need to transplant them. Just hide the pots by topping them with sheet or reindeer moss.

Indoor blooming gardens are nothing more than assemblies of miniature potted plants bearing small blossoms or leaves (like ivy) that you plant in the container of your choice. In fact, your container doesn't even need to be waterproof. Simply line it with plastic, fill it with dirt, pop in your plants, and you're all set.

bringing the outdoors in

Even when the weather is frigid and frosty, there are a number of ways you can invite Mother Nature inside. The most obvious example is to host living trees such as ficus or palm or flowering plants such as orchids or African violets, which have been cultivated to thrive inside. Because we work with—and love—cut flowers, we prefer to bring the outdoors in by creating indoor blooming gardens like the one featured on the preceding pages.

Another version, pictured here, is made to look like a fairy landscape. You can build yours in the traditional manner like a terrarium, which is typically enclosed in a fish tank or fishbowl, or follow our example and "plant" yours in a big bowl. We used a large glass bowl to show off the mix of sand and soil that provides the base for the garden.

None of our flowers is actually rooted in the soil. All are cut. If kept damp like floral foam, the soil will moisten and feed the stems, which will prolong the vase life of the garden. It is easy to keep the garden looking fresh past its prescribed vase life, too; simply replace flowers as they begin to fade. The mosses will keep indefinitely.

A cross between a floral arrangement and a terrarium, our garden-in-a-bowl features tall, furry green amaranthus, plus one spray each of campanula and delphinium. To fill out the arrangement, we've added a few sprays each of raspberry-colored sweet William and green lady's mantle. Ground cover is supplied by clumps of two kinds of moss—reindeer moss and sheet moss—sprinkled with a handful of pebbles.

forcing bulbs

Sometimes we just can't wait until spring's crocuses, daffodils, and tulips come into bloom. Nurseries often get a head start on the season by potting and forcing bulbs in their greenhouses. Because many of their flowering bulbs have to be ready for the winter holidays, they begin the process on the first of October.

Bulbs undergo a two-step process before they flower. Chilling holds them in hibernation at a very cool temperature—between 40 and 50 degrees—for a prescribed number of weeks, to concentrate nutrition and develop strong roots within the bulb. Gradual warming allows the bulb to begin to send out roots and shoots. All this takes time, though—three months or more.

You, too, have to dedicate that much time to force most bulbs in pots, but, luckily, there's one variety—paper whites—that requires no chilling at all. Because of this, paper whites take only three to five weeks to come into bloom. When you purchase bulbs, be sure they are labeled "good for forcing," and check the bulbs for firmness. Their skins should be intact, too, with no visible sprouts. You don't need to pot paper whites either; you can force them in water (see photo opposite) or in a saucer resting on a shallow bed of moist gravel or pebbles. You can also force prechilled hyacinths and crocuses in water.

forcing flowering branches

As the earth warms up, many shrubs and trees begin to send out shoots and buds that eventually burst into bloom. If you prune a shrub bearing plump, ready-to-pop buds, you can accelerate the process. After pruning your branches, split and smash their ends, and thrust them into a pail of warm water augmented with flower food.

Set them in a warm, sunny window and within days—or at most a couple of weeks—you should have a fine bundle of sprays of blossoms. Some flowering branches to consider are quince, apple, crab apple, and cherry.

So, while you're waiting for Mother Nature to have her way, forcing branches and bulbs and creating indoor gardens and terraria can help get you ready for all the wonderful blooms soon to come. Before you know it, more and more flowers will burst into bloom, many of them before your very eyes. And, once that happens, can summer be far behind?

Forcing paper whites in water is easy. Just choose some glass containers for your bulbs; any will do, as long as there's room for roots to expand. (We used drinking glasses here.) Make a crisscross support for the bulb by cutting thin bamboo or twigs to the lengths you need; crisscross them and secure them with dabs of hot glue, or tie them with raffia. Perch your bulbs on top, making sure the base of each bulb rests on water. Roots and shoots should appear the first week; wait another week or two, and voilà! Blooms!

summer

summer
thoughts

Everyone loves the lazy, hazy days of summer—especially when they're on vacation. Fireworks! Hot dogs and hamburgers! Fish fries and clambakes! Fireflies and shooting stars! The sights, sounds, and smells of summer weekends at the lake or beach suffuse the long days and nights with feelings of exhilaration and joy.

Lawns turn lush and gardens brim over to bursting with vibrant, colorful flowers, with more popping into bloom every day. There are so many flowers to choose from, in so many varieties and so many colors, there's absolutely no way you can resist using them in some way, even if it means just tucking one behind your ear. If you are lucky enough to have a garden, a potential flower arrangement blooms mere footsteps from your own back door. Otherwise, florists, farm stands, outdoor markets, and nurseries—and nearby meadows and roadsides—are so replete with flowers, it's hard to decide what to take home.

During the summer, nobody wants to spend too much time arranging flowers. What looks best is a casual, fresh bunch of flowers thrust into a stoneware pitcher or several bundles of blooms cut to fill a collection of jelly jars

or drinking glasses. Our projects for the season are the easiest of the year: mixing strawberries, daisies, and delphinium in a towel-covered container to adorn a picnic table, threading orchid blossoms on monofilament to make a pretty Hawaiian-style lei, and covering a jar with strands of beads to create a sparkly "jeweled" vase. The only project that takes time is one where you wax flowers

before heaping them into a triple-tiered basket—but we think this is such a fun project to do on a rainy day, we couldn't resist sharing it with you.

summertime
gathering
basket

G uess what? You can bring the look of a gloriously colorful cutting garden inside—even if you don't have a garden— by filling baskets with flowers. When displayed as a centerpiece— or as a decoration for any table, indoors or out—our Summertime Gathering Basket invokes the romance of an English-style cottage garden at its peak of perfection.

We assembled our flowers in a trug, the basketlike carrier that English gardeners traditionally use to transport their blooms into the house. A trug is typically crafted of pliable wooden slats bent into the shape of the hull of a boat and stabilized with runners, which prevent it from tipping over. You can, of course, work with any handled basket you like, as long as it has a flat bottom. We inserted our flowers into floral foam so that they'd last a full week rather than merely a day or two; do the same—nobody but you will know!

summertime gathering basket

Queen Anne's lace

French lilac

hydrangeas

delphinium

rose

Level of Difficulty: Easy

Time: ½ hour

Vase Life: 1 week

FLOWERS

2 stems delphinium, 3 stems French lilac, 6 roses, 2 hydrangeas, 2 stems Queen Anne's lace

WHAT YOU NEED

- serrated knife
- 1 brick floral foam
- 1 aluminum loaf-size pan, or black plastic garbage bag
- waterproof elastic floral tape
- trug, or other flat-bottomed, handled basket
- sharp florist's scissors
- cotton dishtowel or napkin
- 4 straight pins

bloomnet®

basics

Pick Queen Anne's lace when blossoms are fully opened; if they are tight, they'll never open. Queen Anne's lace has a tendency to shed, so you may have to replace yours during the vase life of your arrangement.

–C. Brent Conatser
Nashville, TN

1 With the serrated knife, cut the floral foam to fit the pan. Place it in the pan. Crisscross two pieces of elastic floral tape over the floral foam to secure it to the pan. Soak the floral-foam–filled pan thoroughly in water. Pour out the excess water and place the dish in the trug or basket. (If you prefer to use a black garbage bag as your plastic liner, cut it to fit the trug, and place the wet floral foam on top.)

2 Cut the stems of the tallest flowers—in our trug, they are delphinium and French lilac—so that their stems will be long enough to completely fill one-half of the trug. Insert the delphinium and French lilac into the floral foam so that the blossoms drape over the rim of the trug. Save the cut stems and set them aside.

3 Cut the stems of the rest of the flowers, one by one, and insert each in turn into the floral foam, as desired, until they fill one side of the trug.

Step 1. Line trug with black plastic. Cut floral foam to fit aluminum pan; secure to pan with floral tape.

Step 2. Cut flowers to length necessary to start filling one-half of trug; reserve stems. Insert flowers into foam so blossoms drape over rim of trug.

Steps 3–4. Cut remaining flowers and insert in gaps, as desired. Insert all cut stems in foam on opposite side, to appear as if attached to blossoms.

Step 5. Knot dishtowel; rest it on top of cut stems. Attach towel to foam with straight pins, hiding pins under fold in towel.

4 Insert the cut stems that you set aside into the floral foam on the opposite side of the handle, lining them up with the flowers so that they look as if they were still attached to them.

5 Knot the dishtowel or napkin and rest it on top of the cut stems to camouflage where they are inserted into the floral foam. Insert the straight pins through the towel into the floral foam to hold the towel in place, hiding the pins under a fold in the towel.

Quick tip

We knotted our dishtowel and placed it on top of our arrangement midway through the project to give us a sense of where it should be placed and how it would look—then we removed it while we filled out the basket and put it back again when the arrangement was complete.

patriotic berry basket

Oh, say can you see …! One of the high points of summer is Independence Day. Celebrations start with the annual Fourth of July parade and conclude with a traditional down-home barbecue and a shower of fireworks blazing across the sky. On this festive holiday, America's beloved stars-and-stripes pops up everywhere you look: on buntings and garlands and swags, on picnic tablecloths and napkins, and—of course—on the American flags that sparkle on shirts and jacket lapels, unfurl at windows, and fly from flagpoles.

In keeping with the patriotic theme, our charming Americana-style towel-tied berry basket combines a mix of dewy blue delphinium, bright white daisies, and luscious red strawberries in their own spirited striped display. Place several of these baskets on your outdoor picnic cloth or table, and let everyone admire the display. Think of it as a feast for the eyes as well as the taste buds. Be sure to put out a separate bowl of strawberries, too. Someone is sure to want to eat a few!

patriotic berry basket

daisy pom

strawberry

delphinium

Level of Difficulty: Easy
Time: 20 minutes
Vase Life: 4 days

FLOWERS AND FRUIT

8 strawberries, 2 stems delphinium, 2 stems daisy poms

WHAT YOU NEED

- serrated knife

- $\frac{1}{3}$ brick floral foam

- 5-inch-diameter plastic dish or other waterproof container

- waterproof elastic floral tape

- red-and-white cotton dishtowel, napkin, or bandanna, large enough to cover container

- wire cutters

- 6 12-inch-long pieces of medium-gauge florist's wire

- sharp florist's scissors

FRESH thoughts®

If you use flowers instead of strawberries in your patriotic basket, it will last longer—up to 1 week. A couple of long-lasting red flowers to consider are mini-carnations and miniature gerbera daisies.

1 With the serrated knife, cut the floral foam to fit the dish. Place the floral foam in the dish. Crisscross two pieces of elastic floral tape across the floral foam, to secure it to the dish. Soak the floral-foam-filled dish in water.

2 Fold the dishtowel, napkin, or bandanna around the floral-foam-filled plastic dish, making sure to hide the floral foam. Knot the corners of the towel to hold it in place, tucking the edges under the knots for a neat appearance.

3 With wire cutters, cut the wires in half (you will need two each for four strawberries and one each for the remaining strawberries). Insert two cut wires into the top of a strawberry, at right angles to each other; bend and twist the wires together. Repeat the process for three additional strawberries.

Step 1. Cut floral foam to fit dish; attach foam to dish with floral tape. Saturate foam with water.

Step 2. Fold dishtowel around floral-foam-filled dish. Knot corners to hold it in place; pull towel up to hide foam.

Steps 3–4. Cut wires in half. Crisscross and insert two wires in each strawberry, at top or bottom, as desired. (Twist wires together.)

Steps 5–7. Insert strawberries into floral foam at one side of basket. Cut stems of flowers to 3- or 4-inch lengths; insert in foam to fill basket.

4 Insert one wire only through the bottom of one of the remaining strawberries, and bend and twist together the ends of the wire. Repeat with all the remaining strawberries.

5 Insert all the strawberries into the floral foam, forming a cluster of fruit on one side of the container.

6 Cut the stems of delphinium back to yield three or four stems at 3- to 4-inch lengths. Insert these, one by one, into the floral foam, clustering them on the opposite side of the container. Repeat the process for the daisy poms, cutting the individual flowers off their stems to 3- to 4-inch lengths. Insert the poms, one by one, between the delphinium and the strawberries.

7 Adjust the flowers and strawberries, if necessary, so that the entire arrangement looks as if it had been casually piled in the bowl.

waxed tiered delight

How many times have you purchased flowers when they were at their peak—and then wished there were a way to make them last more than a day or two without drying or fading? Well, you can, by waxing them. This method of preserving flowers (and fruit) originated in the Victorian era, and it ensures that your blooms will "live" a full two weeks—and sometimes even longer.

Waxing not only seals the natural moisture within each blossom, but the technique also imparts a lovely patina and sheen. The only thing you have to remember is to let the flower drip off any excess wax, so it can set and harden, before working with it. First, coat all your flowers with paraffin wax, then go ahead and create an artful arrangement, such as this pretty, three-tiered display. To show off our waxed flowers and fruit, we arranged them in a multitiered holder. First we practiced with a two-tiered one, then we changed to one with three tiers because it looked much more luscious. Don't you agree?

waxed tiered delight

Level of Difficulty: Moderate

Time: 1 hour

Vase Life: 2 weeks or more

FLOWERS AND FRUIT

3 stems French lilac, 4 hydrangea, 12 roses, 3 spray roses, 3 Star of Bethlehem, 2 stems statice, 2 bunches grapes

WHAT YOU NEED

- waxed paper

- masking tape

- 2 pounds household paraffin wax, available at the hardware store

- stockpot

- hot plate

- vase to hold flowers until you arrange them

- sharp florist's scissors

- container of your choice to display your waxed flowers

bloomnet®
basics

Household paraffin wax is highly flammable and must be handled with care. Here are some tips to make it easier to work with.

- Be sure your kitchen is well ventilated.

- Do not melt your paraffin wax in a pan directly on the stove. You can melt it in a hot plate or in a tin can in the top half of a double boiler.

- To check that your paraffin wax is not too hot, drop one flower petal into the wax. If the petal curls or discolors—or the wax sizzles—wait a minute before proceeding.

–Linda & Dale Murphy
Lexington, KY

1 Roll out the waxed paper over your work surface. Tape the corners of the waxed paper to the work surface to hold the paper in place.

2 Place the paraffin wax in the stockpot and place the pot on the hot plate. Set the hot-plate thermostat on high. Heat the wax until it is melted (it will turn from cloudy to clear). Turn the thermostat to low to keep the wax warm and liquid.

3 Pick up the first flower by its stem and dip the flower into the melted wax quickly, with a swift in-out motion. When you pull it out, make sure the flower is completely covered with wax. Rotate the flower, turning it until the wax stops dripping, approximately 5 to 10 seconds, then place the flower on the waxed paper to cool. Repeat with all the flowers.

4 Dip clusters of the grapes into melted wax, as above. Rest the grapes on the waxed paper to cool.

Steps 1–2. After taping waxed paper to work surface, heat paraffin wax in stockpot (on hot plate set on high).

Steps 2–3. Turn down hot plate to low. Dip first flower in melted wax, in swift in/out motion. Rotate flower to halt dripping; cool on waxed paper.

Step 5. After waxing all flowers and grapes (step 4), cut flower stems to desired length and arrange flowers and grapes in tiered container.

5 Cut the stems of the flowers to the correct length for your display and arrange the flowers, as desired, in your tiered container. Add the clusters of waxed grapes to fill gaps, allowing them to drape over rim, if desired.

Quick tip

Some waxed flowers, such as fully opened roses, dry best when allowed to stand upright. You have two choices for this.

- Standing in a vase, as pictured here
- Standing in a block of dry floral foam.

hand-tied
bouquets

Bouquets—and their smaller, less ornate cousins, posies and tussy-mussies—are simply bunches of flowers arranged in a round shape so that the blooms can be admired from every angle. To create a bouquet like the two pictured here, all you need to do is gather together the flowers of your choice, tie their stems together, and wrap them securely, either with waterproof elastic floral tape or with ribbon, so that the bouquet is easy to carry.

The pair of bouquets pictured here illustrates two variations on hand-tied bouquets: One is composed of flowers in a mix of compatible hues; the other is monochromatic. Both are accented with ribbon for a pretty touch of softness. We used wired ribbons, which hold their shape more easily than regular ones. Remember, too, that bouquets such as these don't have to be reserved for weddings. A hand-tied bouquet can highlight virtually any special occasion—and it makes a wonderful gift, too.

hand-tied bouquets

rose

Queen Anne's lace

lisianthus

seeded
eucalyptus

Star of
Bethlehem

Level of Difficulty: Moderate

Time: ½ hour

Vase Life: 1 day

FLOWERS AND FOLIAGE FOR THE MULTICOLORED BOUQUET

3 stems alstroemeria, 3 stems delphinium, 4 roses, 4 tulips, 2 stems pittos nigra, 6 stems spray roses

FLOWERS FOR THE MONOCHROMATIC BOUQUET

5 stems lisianthus, 3 stems seeded eucalyptus, 7 Star of Bethlehem, 3 Queen Anne's lace, 2 roses

WHAT YOU NEED

- 1 yard waxed string
- sharp florist's scissors
- 1 yard ribbon, in color of your choice

Quick tip

If you make a bouquet the day before you plan to use it, leave the bottoms of the stems uncovered, so that you can set the bouquet in a vase filled with 1 inch water.

You can also make the bouquet ahead of time and then add the ribbon the next day, closer to the time you will need to use or show off the bouquet.

1 Strip the foliage from the stems of all the flowers.

2 Select a large flower to provide a focus at the center of the bouquet. Using the waxed string, loop the stem of the focal flower twice, 4 inches beneath the flowerhead, leaving the remainder of the string hanging free.

3 Add the next flower, adjusting the bloom so that it barely touches the focal flower; angle its stem at a 45-degree diagonal, and hold the stems tightly where they cross.

4 Turn the bouquet slightly, and add the next two or three flowers in the same way, angling their stems. With the trailing waxed string, loop and bind these stems to the original one, again leaving the remainder of the string hanging free.

5 Repeat with all the flowers, turning the bouquet slightly as you add each flower, angling each stem as you go, mixing blooms as desired, and arranging them so that they form a round or spherical shape. Loop and bind the stems after every two or three flowers you add.

Step 1. Condition all flowers by stripping foliage from their stems, up to the flowerheads.

Step 2. Loop waxed string around stem of focal flower twice, 4 inches beneath flowerhead.

Steps 3–4. Add next flower, angling its stem at 45-degree angle; hold stems tightly where they cross. Add two or three flowers in same way; loop and bind stems together.

6 Once the bouquet has reached the desired fullness, tie the remainder of the string into a tight knot around the angled stems. Cut off the string from the roll.

7 Cut all the stems flat across and to the desired length for the "handle" of your bouquet.

8 Lay the ribbon flat on the worktable and center the bouquet on the ribbon, aligning it with the tops of the stems, under the flowerheads.

9 Bring the two lengths of the ribbon around from behind the stems and crisscross them in front. Pull them around to the back, crisscrossing them again. Repeat crisscrossing, front to back to front, traveling down the bunch of stems until you reach the bottom of the stems (or as far as you want to go). Tie off the ribbon and cut off the excess.

10 Make a floral bow, and tie it to the bouquet at the base of the flowerheads. (To learn how to make a floral bow, turn to our Bloomnet® Basics on page 41.)

Step 5. Continue adding flowers, looping and binding as you go.

Step 6. When bouquet achieves desired fullness, tie off string tightly; cut string off roll.

Step 7. Cut stems across at desired length for "handle" of bouquet.

Steps 8–9. Lay ribbon on work surface; center bouquet on ribbon, at top of stems, under flowerheads. Crisscross ribbons back-to-front and front-to-back, traveling down stems as far as desired.

Step 10. Make floral bow; tie under flowerheads.

bloomnet®
basics

Here are two more ways you can hand-tie ribbons around bouquets.

• If you'd like to expose more of the ribbon on your bouquet, you can start from the top of the stems, underneath the bases of the flowerheads, and crisscross them, as at left, traveling down the stems; tie off, allowing the excess ribbon to hang free; cut the excess ribbon to the desired length and make V-shaped swallow-tails at the ends.

• For a two-toned effect, use two different colored ribbons, layering them one over the other, leaving a slight margin of the lower ribbon for show; crisscross the pair of ribbons up or down the stems, as outlined in our how-tos at left.

–Lynda O'Connor
West Nyack, KY

floral lei

Aloha! Hawaiians greet visitors to their islands by placing one or more leis woven of flowers around their neck and bowing. Leis are worn loosely over the shoulders so that they hang gracefully, both front and back. We love leis and think they are a great substitute for a corsage or a bouquet when acknowledging a special occasion or a special someone, such as the guest of honor at a birthday or retirement party—or a graduating senior. In Hawaii, graduating seniors often receive so many leis they can't see over them!

Our floral lei is made entirely of blooms cut from stems of dendrobium orchids, but you could make yours from any flower—or mix of flowers. In Hawaii, people often mix shells (with holes pierced through them) and feathers and leaves with their blooms to add texture and visual interest to a lei, especially if they want to preserve the lei as a memento. You can, too.

floral lei

dendrobium orchid

Level of Difficulty: Easy

Time: 40 minutes

Vase Life: Up to 1 week, if refrigerated

FLOWERS

6 stems dendrobium orchids (approx. 48 blooms)

WHAT YOU NEED

■ craft or household scissors

■ monofilament or fishing line

■ large embroidery needle

■ sharp florist's scissors

Quick tip

If you don't want to make a trip to the bait and tackle shop for some fishing line, you can also use dental floss for this project. In fact, dental floss will spare you one more item—you won't even need scissors to cut off the length you need!

1 With the craft or house-hold scissors, cut the monofilament or fishing line to the length you want your lei to be, adding 6 inches so that you can tie the ends off to create the lei.

2 Thread the needle with the cut fishing line. Tie a knot about 3 inches from one end of the fishing line to establish a "stopper" at the starting point of your lei.

3 With the florist's scissors, cut a bloom from an orchid stem. Insert the needle through the base of the bloom and gently pull it along the fishing line to the starter knot.

4 Repeat the process for all the blooms, lining them up one with the other so that they rest inside each other with their anthers facing the same direction.

5 When the lei reaches the desired length, tie off the ends of the fishing line in a knot and snip off the excess.

6 Place the lei around the neck of your special someone and say Aloha: Welcome!

Step 3. Cut individual blossoms off spike—or stem—of dendrobium orchid; set aside.

Steps 3–5. Insert needle threaded with fishing line through base of first bloom; pull it along line to starter/stopper knot. Repeat for all blossoms, lining them up so they rest inside each other and anthers face same direction, until lei reaches desired length. Tie off line.

bloomnet®
basics

To store a lei, place it in a plastic grocery bag and put it in the fridge. Orchids absorb moisture through their petals as well as through their stems, so, even without stems, you can still enhance your lei's appearance and extend its vase life by misting it periodically. If you want to preserve your lei for a long time, you might want to consider freeze-drying it. To learn more about this process and where you can get it done, turn to Freeze-Drying Flowers on page 194.

–Georgeanna Spinello
Murrysville, PA

fresh flower present

Anyone will tell you that giving and receiving presents are two of life's greatest pleasures. One popular and traditional gift, of course, is flowers. We can vouch for that.

Gifts that are surprises are the very best of all, don't you think? So, why not give a gift of flowers where the gift itself is created from flowers? What a surprise that will be!

We worked with Santini button poms because they are small and puffy, they hold their shape well, and they can be packed closely together without crushing each other. We also love them because of their fresh, bright green color. To create our Fresh Flower Present, which uses two-thirds of a brick of floral foam, we needed 16 stems of button poms, which gave us the 94 blossoms we required—28 for the top of the brick, 12 for each end, and 21 for each side.

fresh flower present

Santini button pom

Level of Difficulty: Easy
Time: 45 minutes
Vase Life: 1 week

FLOWERS AND LEAVES

16 stems Santini button poms (you will need 94 blossoms; discard extras)

WHAT YOU NEED

- 2 1-yard-long pieces of ribbon, of your choice
- glue gun and glue stick
- 6-inch shallow rectangular plastic tray (the plastic lid off a take-out container works well)
- ⅔ brick floral foam
- waterproof elastic florist's tape
- sharp florist's scissors

Quick tip

Next time you're having a party such as a bridal shower or birthday celebration, why not reciprocate your guests' generosity by giving them each a small fresh flower present as a favor? They also make great presents for moms on Mother's Day, for teachers, or for anyone you'd like to make feel special!

1 Crisscross the ribbons and hot-glue them together where they meet. Add a dab of hot glue to the top of the crisscrossed ribbons where they meet, and press the glue against the underside of the plastic tray to hold the ribbons in place. Flip the tray to an upright position.

2 Thoroughly soak the brick of floral foam in water until saturated. Place the floral foam in the plastic tray.

3 Cut each pom blossom (to a 2-inch length) off a longer stem as you work. Insert the flowers, one by one, Into the floral foam, starting at the base of the brick and working up the sides. Set the blossoms in rows so that the flowers abut each other. Repeat the process until the top and sides of the floral foam are completely covered with blossoms.

4 Pull the ribbons up and tie them into a bow.

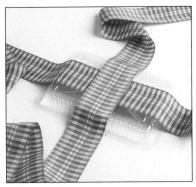

Step 1. Crisscross precut ribbons; hot-glue together where they meet. Hot-glue ribbons to base of plastic tray.

Step 2. Place thoroughly soaked floral foam in tray.

Step 3. Cut poms, one by one, to 2-inch lengths, and, starting at base, set blossoms in row up sides and across top of floral foam. Repeat until floral foam is completely covered.

FRESH thoughts®

You can create your Fresh Flower Present from flowers other than button poms. Just make sure you choose flowers that have firm flower-heads; some flowers to consider are:

- roses in bud
- cushion poms
- mini-carnations.

As with most of our projects, you can try variations of the same theme by mixing blooms if you like—or mix colors of a single variety of flower, such as the rosebuds. It's up to you!

jeweled vase

These beautiful jeweled vases will add dazzle and sparkle to any table at any time of the year. You can fill some with flowers and some with candles—whatever suits your mood or occasion.

Decorating vases with "jewels" is so easy you can even ask the kids to help. (And it'll cut down on bead-assembly time, too.) Tell your helpers how many beads they'll need to make one circle, give them free rein to use their imaginations in their choices of beads, and they'll come running. (We used four sizes of beads in four different colors—lavender, aqua, purple, and clear—and sapphire-colored bugle beads, for contrast, every few rows.)

Buy up bags of translucent beads at your local craft shop and lay them out in saucers, organizing them by size, color, and shape. To assist your little artists, you can measure and cut the thread into pieces; after you thread their needles, they can take over. The needles used are called beading needles; they have long holes in them—and blunt tips so your little beaders' fingers won't get pricked.

jeweled vase

lisianthus

Level of Difficulty: Easy

Time: 1 hour per vase to complete beading

Vase Life: 10 days

FLOWERS

3 stems lisianthus (3 to 5 flowers per stem)

WHAT YOU NEED

- elastic thread
- craft scissors
- 1 3- by 5-inch cylindrical glass container, such as a tumbler or old-fashioned glass
- beading needle
- 250 large beads
- 300 medium beads
- 120 bugle or cylindrical beads
- 720 small beads
- small bowls, to hold beads
- ¼ packet floral preservative
- sharp florist's scissors

Quick tip

We chose beads that would complement the color of our lysianthus, but you can personalize a room or table setting by using any beads you like. Depending upon what flowers you decide to use, you can copy our vase— or choose beads that contrast with the flowers.

Beads can be clear, translucent, or opaque. You can also find beads in other shapes, such as cubes and ellipses. Why not scoop up lots of kinds of beads and keep them on hand for this or other projects? Store them in clear jars so you can identify them easily. Baby food jars are particularly handy for this job.

1 Measure and cut the elastic thread into pieces that will encircle the glass, adding several inches so that you have enough thread to thread the needle and tie off the jeweled "vase bracelet" when it is done.

2 Thread beads onto a piece of elastic thread. Test the bracelet on the glass for fit, and tie it off when you have threaded enough beads to go around the glass. Repeat for every bracelet. You'll need about 80 small beads, 60 medium beads, 40 bugle beads, or 50 large beads to make one bracelet for a vase that's the same size as ours.

3 Arrange the bracelets around your container in any order you desire. We needed 20 bracelets to cover our vase.

4 Fill the vase two-thirds full with water mixed with the floral preservative.

5 With florist's scissors, cut the stems of the lisianthus to the correct length to fit your vase. Arrange the flowers as desired. This type of arrangement looks best when the flowers are tightly clustered.

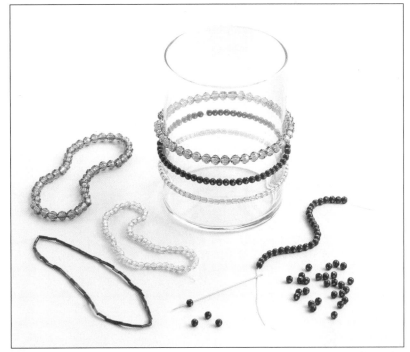

Steps 1–3. Measure and cut elastic thread to lengths that will encircle glass, plus several inches to tie off. Thread first group of beads on piece of elastic thread; test for fit and tie off. Repeat for all beads—until vase is completely covered.

Steps 4–5. Fill vase two-thirds full with water mixed with floral preservative. Cut stems of lisianthus to correct length to fit vase; arrange and cluster blooms in vase, as desired.

nature's window

When you're in a hurry and want to make a dramatic flower statement, here's a great new idea we borrowed from the galleries we visited at the latest international flower shows. This trendy, modern design showcases the entire flower—including the stem and head—inside the container. It's an incredibly easy way to pull together a stylish look that's modern and elegant in a flash.

This arrangement is only a start. You can follow our lead or create your own variations of our "window" and display them in many ways. One idea is to run several vases of the same size—or different sizes—down the length of a table instead of using a standard centerpiece. Or place a vase or two on a windowsill that faces the sun, allowing the light from outside to shine through the vase and through the blossoms of the flowers. It's better than a stained-glass window. And passersby are sure to take notice, too.

nature's window

calla lily

Level of Difficulty: Easy
Time: 20 minutes
Vase Life: 7–10 days

FLOWERS

12 calla lilies

WHAT YOU NEED

■ 30-inch-high clear glass vase with a 10-inch opening

■ ½ packet floral preservative

■ florist's scissors

FRESH thoughts®

Calla lilies aren't the only flowers that would look good in Nature's Window. Another flower to consider is the French tulip; these have longer stems than standard tulips, so you can cut them to different lengths to fit the vase. You can also try a more theatrical bloom, such as bird-of-paradise.

1 Pour 2 (or 3) inches of water into the vase and add the floral preservative. Cut the calla lily stems to varying lengths, as desired.

2 Position the shortest calla lilies in the vase, crisscrossing their stems.

3 Repeat with all your flowers, adding them by height and inserting the tallest last.

Quick tip

The design we have suggested here is just one way to arrange these flowers. You can experiment with other ideas. For example, cut all the flowers to the same length for another dramatic look.

Step 1. Pour 2 to 3 inches of water into vase and add floral preservative. Cut stems of calla lilies to varying lengths.

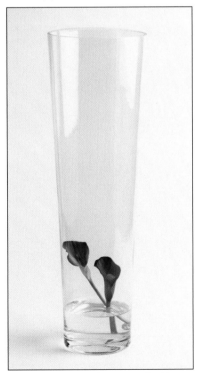

Step 2. Position shortest calla lilies in vase first, crisscrossing their stems.

Step 3. Add calla lilies, one by one, by height, crisscrossing stems, until arrangement is complete.

wedding
proposals

Weddings are like fairy tales. At 1-800-FLOWERS®, we feel lucky because we get to celebrate weddings all year round, not just once in a lifetime— especially now that weddings seem to be taking place virtually any time, anywhere. June's still the most popular month, though, followed closely by May, September, and October. Eighty percent of all brides also still opt for a formal wedding.

There are so many ways flowers can be carried or displayed to make the day truly unforgettable, we can barely count them all! There's the bridal bouquet, of course, as well as bouquets for the bridesmaids. These days, the bride's and groom's mothers sometimes carry small bouquets (called nosegays or tussie-mussies), too, instead of wearing corsages. Also on the must-have list are boutonnieres for the men in the wedding party, flowers for the ceremony and the reception, gifts of flowers for the families of the bride and groom, flower baskets for the flower girls, the toss bouquet the bride throws before she and the groom leave on their honeymoon—the list goes on and on.

White calla lilies are one of nature's most dramatic and beautiful flowers. That's why more and more brides are asking to carry them instead of a conventional mixed-flower bouquet. Calla lilies look especially wonderful in contemporary settings, but they can provide theatrical flair in a more traditional setting, too.

what to ask
your florist

Even if it's just for this one day, you and your florist are like a married couple, too. You are making one of the most important decisions of your life with this pro, so you want to see eye-to-eye. This is one time in your life you don't want any surprises, so you should shop around before choosing the right florist for you. Ask other brides for their recommendations, and ask the manager of the place where you will have your reception for florists he recommends, too.

We often suggest that the bride (and her mother) drop in unannounced at the various florists they are considering, to observe firsthand how they work. Here are some questions to ask before settling on a specific florist.

• What kinds of weddings has the florist worked on before? Ask to see photos of other weddings he has done, with close-ups of bouquets and other arrangements, to see if your tastes and styles mesh. Ask to see if he is working on any wedding displays when you visit, to give you an idea of what he is doing at that moment.

• Is the florist familiar with the locations you've chosen for the ceremony and reception? If he is, perhaps he has some ideas that have worked well in the past.

• How much will all this cost? Be clear and specific about what you can spend. One way to keep costs down is to use flowers that are in season.

• Bring pictures of the wedding dress and bridesmaids' dresses, plus swatches of the fabrics, if possible. If you can, bring in pictures of the dresses the bride's mother and groom's mother will wear, too. And bring in some paint chips of colors you like, to give the florist a sense of your taste.

• Cut out magazine photos of bouquets and other arrangements you particularly like (and dislike) and bring these along so the florist can have some visual clues to get an idea of what you want.

Once you've settled on your florist, the fun begins. As florists, one thing we always try to do is set aside a quiet place, away from the hubbub of our flower-arranging center, so we can give our undivided attention to our wedding clients. You should insist on this as well. Here are a few hints to help you arrive at a decision about what flowers will work best for your wedding.

- Make a master list of all the flower arrangements you want to include. Your florist may suggest additional ideas, but you should let him know what the "must have" arrangements are for your special day.

- What time is the wedding to be held? Is it going to be indoors or outside? You want flowers that will hold up all day.

- Ask the florist to come up with a number of options—with samples—so you can make an informed choice about the look you want. Samples may cost a bit extra, but it is worth it to know what you are getting. You can also ask if you can drop by and see samples of work he's doing for someone else's wedding.

When you come to an agreement, find out what your latest date is to make any changes. Typically, a florist doesn't order the flowers until a week or two before the wedding, so you should have plenty of time to make any last-minute substitutions.

bouquet styles

Bridal bouquet trends have changed over the years; now there's a wide range of styles to choose from to match or offset the style and mood of the wedding gown. A wedding bouquet should complement—not overshadow—the wedding dress, so it's best to post-pone any floral decisions until you know the style and color of the gown. Certain colors for flowers have become popular, too, such as rich ruby red, deep rose, burgundy, and

violet, which may be used instead of traditional all-white. Also, remember to consider how tall or small you are. The bouquet shouldn't overwhelm the bride, but it shouldn't look skimpy either. How big a bouquet do you want to carry? Ask to test a sample bouquet to see how it feels and looks. Bridal bouquet styles run the gamut. Here are several to choose from to suit your personality:

Cascade *(Traditional)*

For years, the traditional bouquet has been a formal, cascading type. In this flowing arrangement, the flowers drape over the bride's clasped hands like a waterfall. Cascades especially suit all-white or

white-and-green arrangements where flowers and leaves display a variety of textures. Cascades are often accented with strings of beads or pearls.

Presentation *(Free-Spirited)*

A much more colorful and carefree arrangement, the Presentation Bouquet mixes lots of different flowers in a wide range of colors and textures. One advantage of this type of bouquet is that it goes with dresses of every hue, so you don't have to worry about matching it with every fabric worn by members of the wedding party—or guests, for that matter. Presentation Bouquets are usually carried in the crook of the arm.

Romantic *(Sentimental)*

Like Cascade and Presentation Bouquets, the Romantic Bouquet assembles a variety of flowers, but these are softer and more delicate in terms of color and texture. Romantic Bouquets are usually hand-tied, like those on page 123. Some or all of the flowers may be scented and imbued with special sentiments like sweetness, devotion, and hope. Brides typically carry Romantic and Tassel-Tied Bouquets clasped in both hands.

Tassel-Tied *(Dramatic)*

A variation on Presentation and Hand-Tied Bouquets, the Tassel-Tied Bouquet pulls together a variety of dramatic blooms in strong colors that are offset by white flowers and green foliage for a theatrical effect. The bouquet also juxtaposes spiky flowers with softer flowers, such as roses, bearing velvety petals. Tassels hang free at the bottom of the stems.

Quick tip

The Toss—or Throw-Away—Bouquet is a small version of the bridal bouquet, which the bride tosses into the crowd when she and the groom are ready to leave the reception. Many brides ask for a separate Toss Bouquet so that they can preserve the bridal bouquet as a keepsake of their special day. Some florists will make up a Toss Bouquet, gratis; ask!

head wreaths and corsages

Sometimes brides as well as flower girls wear head wreaths, like the one pictured with our Presentation Bouquet on page 148. Head wreaths can be lush and full like this one, or they may be very delicate, threading a few blooms and greens along florist's spool wire or monofilament for a dainty look.

The most important thing to remember, of course, is fit. Measure the head of the person who'll be wearing the wreath, and give the measurement to your florist so he can be sure to make it just the right size. You will also have to let your florist know if you'd like to attach a veil, cut organza or tulle, so it can be sewn to the underside of the wreath.

Corsages are usually worn by other women in the wedding party, such as the mothers of the bride and groom, grandmothers, and aunts. Corsages can be worn in a number of ways: pinned to a dress, encircling the wrist, or attached to a handbag. Ask the wearers which way would feel most comfortable. Some dress fabrics, like silk, are delicate and would be marred by pinholes.

Stephanotis is very popular mixed in bridal bouquets. But it can also make a pretty bouquet all on its own. One way to highlight stephanotis is with pearl-headed pins like those used to hold corsages. Florists also carry special Q-tiplike sticks with flat tips made of felt, which are pushed up through the flowers to steady their tender stems. The pins are pushed through the center of the blooms into the felt to secure them.

FRESH thoughts®

White Flowers

Traditionally, brides have carried bouquets of white flowers, as a symbol of innocence and purity. These days, weddings that feature all-white flower arrangements are called "champagne weddings." Here are some of our favorite white flowers, which you can use alone, mixed with foliage, or with other flowers that you love.

- baby's breath
- bouvardia
- calla lily
- camellia
- carnation
- chrysanthemum
- delphinium
- dendrobium orchid
- freesia
- french lilac
- gardenia
- hydrangea
- jasmine
- lily
- lily-of-the-valley
- lisianthus
- orange blossom
- paper white
- peony
- rose
- stephanotis
- stock
- tuberose
- tulip
- white lilac

innovative wedding ideas

Unexpected floral touches are wonderful ways to personalize a wedding. Why not tie chair corsages on the chairs set aside for the bride and groom and on pews in the church? Or use wheat grass as a "lawn" for place cards as we did here, and complement it with sparkling silver julep cups filled with tufts of the glossy green grass. (Wheat grass is especially stylish because its blades are thick and flat and it stands up just like a crew cut.) Or use multiples of the same type of container, such as shot glasses, to hold lots of tiny tea candles as well as tiny bunches of flowers. Standard votive candleholders, too, can be teamed with flowers, as long as the blossoms are small and firm. And tall candlesticks can be wreathed or garlanded with leaves and flowers to coordinate with long taper candles—in whatever hues you like best. Light and color—that's what weddings are all about. That, and love!

FRESH thoughts®

One of our favorite floral designers is Jane Carroll. Jane has designed many weddings and is especially known for her unique floral fashion sense, such as this evening bag that she's covered in soft, overlapping sage-green lamb's ears and trimmed with flowers—perfect for a bride or even for bridesmaids. She has also decorated high-heeled shoes—and even mannequins—with flowers to use as centerpieces.

What Jane does best is let her imagination run free—and flowers help her along the way. Some of Jane's other ideas, such as filling little boxes with miniature blossoms to give away as party favors or bundling bunches of all-of-a-kind blooms in tiny urns and clustering them on the table instead of centerpieces, are beautiful—and unique—ways to help make your special day unforgettable.

Wedding flowers have never been so varied nor so important to the mood of the occasion. Just as wedding dress styles change, so do floral trends. One trend is to mix together flowers that have special meaning, such as roses, which say, "I love you," and stephanotis, which signifies good luck and happiness in marriage; another is to include flowers with a wonderful perfume, such as freesia or sweet peas or orange blossoms. The major trend is to coordinate all flowers, from altarpieces to centerpieces.

At weddings, flowers show up everywhere you look: on and around the cake, on the cake knife, on serving plates, on place cards—as well as on the tables, chandeliers, and specially built architectural elements, such as columns and arches that decorate the party space. What would weddings be without flowers? We simply can't imagine it!

fall

fall
thoughts

With the onset of fall, the air grows crisp and cool. The sky looks brighter, clearer, and bluer than blue. Trees begin to turn, sending out one or two red, orange, and yellow leaves, then more and more and more, until they are completely mantled in color. This is the season for long walks through the falling leaves or for raking them into piles—and jumping in them, too! Now, everywhere you go, you can smell fire smoke curling from chimneys, and your cheeks redden from the hint of chill that's in the air.

For many people, fall marks beginnings and fresh starts—like the New Year. After the slow pace of summer, everyone takes a deep breath and plunges into the season with renewed vigor. Work starts up after a well-earned vacation. Sweaters and overcoats come out of their mothballs. The first day of school gets the whole family excited, and apples are polished for the teacher—for this is, after all, the season of harvest, of apples, pears, gourds, squashes, and pumpkins galore. Later, after the merriment of Halloween, the season turns to turkeys and pies and Thanksgiving, when the whole family gathers and everyone goes all out to cook and bake—and make beautiful centerpieces for the table.

Nature's palette relaxes after the hot, vibrant colors of summer. Leaves, pods, grasses, and blooms appear earthier, more muted in tone. Many of our projects this season center on everlastings, which feature dried flowers and plant materials that will last into the winter—and beyond. One project, a floral drying rack, allows your chosen blooms to air-dry on their own. Others, like our harvest swag and overflowing cornucopia, combine fresh and dried flowers, but they could just as easily be all fresh or all dried. It's entirely up to you.

harvest garland

Cascades of fruits and flowers like the ones tumbling down this Harvest Garland seem to embody all the riches of Nature. It's no wonder, then, that a luxuriant display such as this perfectly complements Fall's most festive holiday: Thanksgiving. This is the one feast of the season—and, indeed, of the entire year—that not only gathers family from far and near, but also celebrates food in all its variety and abundance.

One way you might consider sharing the work, and the pleasure, of getting ready for the occasion is to create Harvest Garlands and other decorations—and food!—as communal projects with your family or friends. "Many hands make light work," the saying goes. It's a lovely way to have fun, too.

And then, of course, it's time to eat!

harvest garland

yarrow

preserved oak leaves

lemon leaf

seeded eucalyptus

safflower

Level of Difficulty: Moderate to Difficult

Time: 2 hours

Vase Life: Fresh—up to 2 weeks; Dried—from 4 to 6 weeks

FLOWERS AND FRUIT

3 stems safflower, 7 stems yarrow, 4 stems seeded eucalyptus, 8 stems lemon leaf, 6 stems preserved oak leaves (available from a craft shop—or to find out how to preserve your own, see Preserving Oak Leaves on page 197), 9 small apples

WHAT YOU NEED

■ sharp florist's scissors

■ 18 pieces 12-inch-long medium-gauge florist's wire, for flowers

■ sharp household scissors

■ 1-inch-wide green floral stem wrap

■ 6 feet waxed florist's thread or heavy-gauge spool wire

■ 18 pieces 12-inch-long fine-gauge florist's wire, for apples

■ 36 3-foot-long pieces raffia

Quick tips

Garlands can work in any room in the house. Here are some tips to keep in mind when creating your garland.

• The secret to a lush-looking garland is to make it with clusters of flowers and leaves, mixed together, rather than single blooms and leaves.

• When you make a garland, take its size and length into account ahead of time. The thicker and longer the garland is, the heavier it will be, so be sure that whatever you hang it from can bear the weight.

1 With the florist's scissors, cut the blossoms from the stems of safflower and yarrow, and sprigs of seeded eucalyptus and lemon leaves from their stems, to 3-inch lengths. Separate the flowers by variety, and set them aside.

2 Gather together one or two safflowers with one or two preserved oak leaves and a lemon leaf. Wire the stems by winding the medium-gauge wire from the top of the stem, under the flowerhead (or leaf), to the end. Twist together the ends of the wire. Repeat the process for all the flowers (including the yarrow and seeded eucalyptus) and lemon leaves, mixing them in different combinations.

3 With the household scissors, cut 1-foot strips of floral stem wrap—enough strips for every cluster of flowers and leaves. (We made our garland with 18 clusters, which requires 18 strips of stem wrap.)

4 Using a strip of green stem wrap, tape a bunch of the stems together. Let the excess tape hang off the ends of the stems. Repeat for every cluster of flowers and leaves.

Steps 1–3. Cut and gather preserved oak leaves, flower stems, and sprigs into clusters of three to five pieces each. Wire each cluster.

Step 4. Bind each cluster of leaves and blooms with stem wrap, leaving excess tape dangling.

Step 5. Attach first cluster to one end of wire (or waxed florist's thread) by wrapping excess tape around wire; repeat with all clusters, from top to bottom of wire.

5 Attach the first bunch of stems to one end of the 6-foot-long piece of waxed florist's thread or heavy-gauge wire by wrapping the excess tape around the thread. Repeat with all the clusters, working from the top of the garland to the bottom until you achieve the look you want.

6 Wire the apples (see Wiring Fruit on page 196) and attach them to the garland, either singly or in clusters, spacing them evenly along the length of the garland.

7 Tie the strands of raffia into a bow; add extra if you are going to attach the garland to the wall or other surface, so you can make a loop to hang it from.

Step 6. Wire apples; twist wires on each apple together. Attach wired apples to garland, singly or in clusters, along garland.

fresh sunflower wreath

Originating in ancient times as a decorative headdress called a diadem, the wreath was worn as a mark of status and royalty. By the 15th century, wreaths, both for the head and for the home, had evolved into symbols of joy and were used to celebrate holidays and festivals—as they are today. You can make wreaths to celebrate any occasion you like—use flowers and appropriate decorative elements to match the occasion. Like Chair Corsages (see page 79), wreaths can be hung from the backs of chairs pulled up to a dinner table, or they may be used as centerpieces on the table itself. Or put them anywhere, for that matter.

Wreaths can be fresh and seasonal, as here, or made to last year-round. For the base, you have a number of options: floral foam, straw, grapevine, or chicken wire covered with moss. Choose the base that works best for you. We used floral foam because we wanted to keep our fresh flowers moist. To learn more about fresh and dried wreaths—and to find out more about how to make them—turn to the Winter Seasonal Specialty on page 245.

fresh sunflower wreath

Level of Difficulty: Easy to moderate

Time: 1 hour

Vase Life: Fresh—up to 2 weeks; dried—up to 1 month

FLOWERS AND LEAVES

3 stems lemon leaf, 2 stems seeded eucalyptus, 2 stems pitto nigra, 4 small sunflowers, 25 stems button poms, 3 stems yarrow, 2 stems statice, 2 stems solidago, 2 stems preserved oak leaves (available from a craft shop—or to find out how to preserve your own, see Preserving Oak Leaves on page 197), 3 stems wheat

WHAT YOU NEED

- 12-inch-diameter floral-foam ring

- sharp florist's scissors

- 12 3-foot-long pieces raffia

- 6 fern pins

bloomnet®
basics

Puncturing the floral-foam wreath base too often can cause it to crumble and fall apart. To avoid this mishap, choose the positions of all your flowers—particularly larger stemmed flowers like our sunflowers—*before* inserting them.

–Russ & Terri Kleismit AIFD
Osprey, FL

1 Thoroughly soak the floral-foam ring in water.

2 With the florist's scissors, cut the blossoms of all the flowers off their stems and the leaves off theirs, to 2-inch lengths. Separate the flowers by variety, and set them aside.

3 Insert the lemon leaves around the hole and the outside perimeter of the floral-foam ring to create a foundation for the wreath.

4 Sparingly add seeded eucalyptus and pitto nigra, filling in the basic shape until you establish the overall width of the wreath. Don't be too heavy-handed at this point. You need to leave room for your flower inserts.

5 Insert the sunflowers, spacing them at three points on the ring—more or less at 12-, 4-, and 8-o'clock positions on the wreath.

6 Fill in the wreath with the remaining flowers—button poms, statice, yarrow, and solidago—spacing them as desired. Add the oak leaves, more lemon leaves, and the wheat, wherever there is a gap.

Steps 3–4. Insert lemon leaves into water-saturated floral-foam wreath form. Add seeded eucalyptus and pitto nigra, as desired.

Step 5. Insert sunflowers at 12-, 4-, and 8-o'clock positions on wreath.

Step 6. Insert remaining flowers and leaves in gaps between sunflowers until wreath achieves desired fullness.

7 Twist three or four pieces of raffia together; lace the twisted raffia in and out of the flowers and leaves, securing the ends with fern pins. Repeat the process with the rest of the raffia strips, if desired.

Quick tip

Take advantage of the hollow at the center of your wreath and fill it with a hurricane lamp or a fat pillar candle. You can also place a bowl of fruit in the hole. For a festive dinner, why not make a number of different-sized wreaths and scatter them over the tabletop? Place your serving dishes in them and let your guests help themselves, family style.

Step 7. Twist strips of raffia together; lace in and out of flowers and leaves; secure raffia with fern pins.

floral drying rack

This winsome yet sophisticated wall decoration is created from preserved blossoms, plus "rungs" made from fragrant cinnamon sticks. Preserved flowers last a lot longer than flowers that stand in water. Our Floral Drying Rack not only is pretty, but it also demonstrates the easiest way to preserve flowers, which is to air-dry them. Tie up one or two—or a small bundle (but no more than a half-dozen)—of each type of flower you want to display, then hang them on the cinnamon rungs of the rack. You can, of course, add as many rungs—and flowers—as you want to your own drying rack. The main thing to remember is to leave plenty of room around the flowers so the air can freely circulate.

Floral drying racks look wonderful against a textured wall, as pictured here, but you can hang them almost anywhere—in a window (though flowers will fade in the sun and need to be replaced), from a ceiling beam, from a shelf, or anyplace that has decent air circulation. Find a spot that suits you, measure for fit, and go for it!

floral drying rack

rose • safflower • solidago • delphinium • spray rose • caspia • statice • statice

Level of Difficulty: Easy
Time: 40 minutes
Vase Life: Months

FLOWERS AND PLANT MATTER

3 12-inch-long cinnamon sticks

For top rung, left to right: 1 rose, 1 stem delphinium, and 1 stem spray roses

For second rung: 1 stem purple statice, 1 stem caspia, and 1 stem red statice

For bottom rung: 1 rose tied with 1 stem caspia, 1 stem solidago, and 1 stem safflower

WHAT YOU NEED

■ sharp florist's scissors

■ 9 thin rubber bands

■ 9 10-inch-long pieces raffia, plus 6 3-yard-long strips raffia

FRESH thoughts®

Our floral drying rack is a decorative piece that we hope you will enjoy anywhere in your home. The main thing to remember is that direct sun may cause your blooms to fade prematurely. Humidity may cause them to mold before they have a chance to dry, too, so hanging a drying rack in a bathroom may not be a good idea.

1 With the florist's scissors, cut back the stems of the fresh flowers to the length you desire. Remove all the leaves from the stems.

2 To assemble a bundle of flowers, lay out several blooms so that their blossoms barely touch one another and secure their stems with a thin, flexible rubber band. Repeat for every bundle of flowers.

3 Tie a 10-inch-long strip of raffia around the rubber band of each bundle of flowers, allowing the excess to hang free.

4 Twist several strands of 3-yard-long raffia together to form one thicker strip. Repeat the process to form a second strip. Tie one end of each strip together into a knot to create the "hanger" for the rack. Measure 12 inches down the strips; loop and tie the raffia around the ends of the first cinnamon stick to form the first rung. Leave the raffia hanging loose. Tie the other end of each raffia strip to each end of the first cinnamon stick to form the top rung.

5 Repeat the process in step 4 to create the second and third rungs of the drying rack, making sure you leave enough space between each rung to hang the flowers you've chosen.

6 Tie three bundles of flowers to each rung, spacing them as desired. Cut off the excess raffia when the rack is complete.

Steps 1–3. Cut flowers to desired length; remove leaves from stems. Secure bunches of blossoms with rubber bands. Tie raffia around each rubber band to conceal it. Leave excess raffia hanging free.

Steps 4 and 6. Twist several strands of 3-yard-long strips of raffia to form two thicker strips. Tie strips together to form knot, to hang rack; measure 12 inches on each strip; loop and tie raffia around ends of first cinnamon stick to form rung. Tie three bunches of flowers to rung.

Steps 5 and 6: Repeat steps 4 (minus hanger) and 6, as above, spacing bunches of flowers on rungs as desired, until rack is complete. Cut off excess raffia.

autumn
cornucopia

The *cornu copiae*, which means horn of plenty in Latin, originated as a goat's horn, curved at its tip, which was filled to overflowing with ears of grain and fruit to signify nature's everlasting gifts of abundance. To us, the cornucopia is still a wonderful emblem of autumn and especially of Thanksgiving, when families and friends come together to share a meal that celebrates nature's blessings.

To make a cornucopia, twist a cone from chicken wire, flip it up at its tip, and wrap it tightly with galax leaves and moss, which are hot-glued in place. When you're done, place your cornucopia on a sideboard or at the center of your table—or wherever you plan on displaying it—and fill it to bursting with fall flowers and fruits. When your family and friends arrive, your cornucopia will immediately let them know that your affection for them is as bountiful as the horn of plenty itself.

autumn cornucopia

Level of Difficulty: Moderate to Difficult

Time: 1½ hours

Vase Life: 2 weeks

FLOWERS, MOSSES, VINES, AND LEAVES

2 market bunches galax leaves, approx. 11- by 14-inch piece sheet moss, 2 stems grapevine, 3 stems seeded eucalyptus, 3 stems spray roses, 4 stems French lilac, 2 stems solidago, 1 stem euphorbia, 2 stems hypericum, 5 roses

VEGETABLES AND FRUIT

1 artichoke, 3 apples, 1 bunch red grapes

WHAT YOU NEED

■ 48-inch-long piece of 13-inch-wide medium-gauge chicken wire, folded in half (this double-thick piece of chicken wire will now measure 24 inches long)

■ 1 brick floral foam

■ 1 6- by 11-inch plastic dish or tray (approximately the same size as the brick of floral foam)

■ glue gun and glue sticks

■ sharp florist's scissors

■ 4 6-inch-long florist's sticks

■ 12-inch-long piece medium-gauge florist's wire

FRESH thoughts®

Stems lengths will vary widely according to how far the various flowers spread out from the opening of the horn. To keep track, eyeball each flower separately against the ones that are already in place before making any cuts. That way you will know exactly how long a stem will have to be to reach all the way to the floral foam; then add 2 inches more so you can insert the stem into the floral foam.

1 Bend the double-thick piece of chicken wire into a horn shape, tilting it upward at its tip. Secure the seam of the form by bending back the cut ends of chicken wire and twisting them under each other.

2 Place the brick of floral foam in the plastic tray. Soak the floral-foam–filled tray in water, then place it in the mouth of the cornucopia.

3 With the glue gun, hot-glue the back of a galax leaf at its base, near the stem. Attach the leaf to the chicken-wire form. Repeat the process until the entire form is covered with leaves, making sure each leaf overlaps the previous one.

4 Tear the sheet moss into pieces and hot-glue the pieces here and there on top of the galax leaves to create a random mossy look.

5 Twist the grapevine around the horn, as desired.

6 With the florist's scissors, cut the stems of the seeded eucalyptus to 3-inch lengths. Insert them along the bottom front edge of the floral foam to create the base of the cornucopia.

Steps 1–2. Bend double-thick piece of chicken wire into horn shape. Secure with wire. Place soaked floral foam in cornucopia.

Step 3. Hot-glue back of galax leaf at base; attach to chicken-wire form. Repeat with all leaves, overlapping them, to cover form.

Step 4. Tear sheet moss into pieces; hot-glue to cornucopia, where desired.

Steps 6–8. Insert seeded eucalyptus along mouth of cornucopia. Cut remaining flowers; add to arrangement. Pierce apples and artichokes with floral sticks; add to arrangement.

7 Cut blossoms and sprigs of the remaining flowers—spray roses, French lilac, solidago, euphorbia, and hypericum—off their stems, to 3- to 6-inch lengths. One by one, add each to the cornucopia as you cut it, building up the display layer by layer. Mass the flowers as desired, until they cascade in a way that appeals to you. Insert the five roses last, placing them wherever they look best. (Stem lengths will vary; see Fresh Thoughts® on the opposite page.)

8 Pierce the base of the artichoke and each apple with a floral stick. Insert the apples and artichoke into the floral foam, wherever you want to feature them in the cornucopia.

9 Bend the 12-inch-long piece of medium-gauge florist's wire into a U and insert the wire through the stem of the grapes. Twist the ends of the wire together, and insert it into the floral foam, where desired.

nature's vase

Because they are both born and bred in the garden, vegetables and flowers complement each other beautifully in many arrangements and displays, especially when the vegetable stands in for a traditional container. Autumn offers a veritable treasure trove of potential containers: pumpkins, gourds, and thick-skinned squashes are the most obvious. (In the summer, you can use thick-skinned melons, such as watermelon.) Not only are the squashes colorful, but they come in wonderful and whimsical shapes. Many of them are watertight—at least for the duration of the vase life of the blooms you put in them.

With its long neck and rotund belly, the butternut squash pictured here is one of the most appealing of all squashes. Butternut is exceptionally strong; in fact, it is so sturdy, it can be difficult to cut. If you find a standard kitchen knife hard to handle, try one with a serrated blade instead. That should do the trick.

nature's vase

seeded
eucalyptus

Asiatic lily

solidago

hypericum

Level of Difficulty: Easy
Time: ½ hour
Vase Life: 1 week

FLOWERS AND VEGETABLES

approximately 8-inch-tall butternut squash with an upright
neck, 3 stems Asiatic lily, 3 stems seeded eucalyptus,
4 stems hypericum, 2 stems celosia, if available, or solidago

WHAT YOU NEED

- large, sharp kitchen knife
- large spoon or ice cream scoop
- ⅓ brick floral foam
- serrated knife
- sharp florist's scissors
- 1 6-inch-long floral stick

Quick tip

The pollen on the stamens
of Asiatic lilies can stain
if the stamens come into
contact with clothes or
skin. They can be removed
by pinching them off at
the stem with a paper
towel in hand.

    If you do get a stain on
your clothes, it can often be
removed by dry-brushing
it with a hairbrush or
gently rubbing a piece
of velvet ribbon or a pipe
cleaner over it. The latter
two are your best bets
because you can dispose
of them afterward.

1 With the kitchen knife, cut off the top of the squash, about 1½ inches from the stem. Save the top.

2 Cut into the squash to loosen the pulp, taking care that you do not pierce the skin on the sides of the squash. With the spoon or ice cream scoop, extract the flesh, pulp, and seeds from inside the squash, leaving about ½-inch thickness of flesh next to the skin.

3 Soak the floral foam in water. Place the wet floral foam into the cavity of the squash, trimming with the serrated knife to fit if necessary.

4 With the florist's scissors, cut one blossom off a stem of the Asiatic lily, to stand at the center of the arrangement and serve as its focus. Insert it into top of the floral foam. Cut the rest of the lilies and insert them into the floral foam to establish the parameters of the overall shape you desire.

5 Cut sprigs of the seeded eucalyptus and insert them into the floral foam, starting at the lip of the opening of the squash and filling in the entire shape.

Steps 1–2. Cut off top of squash. Scoop out pulp, seeds, and flesh of squash, leaving 1-inch thickness of flesh next to squash skin.

Steps 3–4. Stuff water-soaked floral foam into squash cavity. Cut and insert Asiatic lily in floral foam, for focal point. Cut and insert other lilies.

Steps 5–7. Cut all flowers into sprigs; insert into foam to fill gaps. Insert one-half floral stick into squash top; insert at base of arrangement, if desired.

6 Cut sprigs of the hypericum and celosia or solidago to 3-inch lengths, one by one, and fill in the gaps in the arrangement, as desired.

7 (optional): Break the floral stick in half and insert one piece into the top of the squash. Insert the top into the floral foam at the base of the arrangement, for added visual interest.

FRESH thoughts®

Winter squash are thicker skinned than summer varieties. Besides commonplace types such as the butternut used in our project, and hubbards and acorns, check out less familiar varieties, which include rotund amber cups, top-knotted red-orange-and-green speckled turk's turbans, all-white cream of the crops, and green buttercups. And, don't forget pumpkins in all sizes!

country blooms

Country means a lot of things to a lot of people. To some, it is a place. To others, it is a state of mind. For florists like us, it signifies a bit of both. Flowers that look as if they'd been freshly picked from the roadside or a field are reminders of a special place, even if it's merely a place you remember from a past visit out of town. For our arrangement, we experimented with different types of hydrangea; some have fat full petals, while others have much smaller petals that look almost like those of viburnum. Either way, the texture and lovely round shape of hydrangea should be a part of a collection of country blooms.

A container such as our milk can is a well-loved emblem of the "country style," a way of decorating that is relaxed and informal and easy to live with. Another might be a milk churn—or, indeed, a miniature version of a real barrel. So, why not follow our example and bring the spirit of country indoors? It's a great way to celebrate fall.

country blooms

hydrangea

rose

sunflower

safflower

solidago

euphorbia

Level of Difficulty: Easy
Time: 45 minutes
Vase Life: 1 week

FLOWERS AND FOLIAGE

3 twigs, 4 hydrangeas, 4 euphorbia, 5 roses,
4 stems safflower, 4 stems solidago, 4 sunflowers,

WHAT YOU NEED

- vase or glass container that will fit the milk can or firkin

- ½ packet floral preservative

- milk can, found at flea markets and antique fairs

- pruning shears

- glue gun and hot glue

- sharp florist's scissors

Quick tip

The easiest way to water an arrangement like this one—or any arrangement for that matter—is with a small watering can with a long, narrow spout, because the spout can easily penetrate clusters of blooms.

1 Fill the glass container three-fourths full with water and add the floral preservative. Insert the container inside the milk can.

2 With the pruning shears, cut the twigs to a length that will cover the opening of your container. Crisscross the twigs across the opening to create a grid.

3 Hot-glue the grid of crisscrossed twigs to the rim of the opening.

4 With the florist's scissors, cut the stems of the hydrangea with its leaves that will stand at the center of the arrangement, to a length that will reach the water in the container. Position these within the central opening in the twiggy grid.

5 Repeat the process with the rest of your flowers— the euphorbia, roses, safflower, solidago, and sunflowers— cutting them one by one and filling in the openings in the grid, as desired, to create a free-flowing, loose bundle of flowers.

Step 1. Fill glass container three-quarters full with water; add floral preservative. Place container inside milk can.

Steps 2–3. Prune twigs to fit opening in can; crisscross and hot-glue twigs across opening to create grid.

Steps 4–5. Cut and position hydrangeas in grid. Repeat for all flowers, filling grid openings, to complete arrangement.

FRESH thoughts®

Most of the flowers featured in our Country Blooms arrangement, namely the hydrangeas, roses, safflowers, and solidago, air-dry well. So, once the other flowers in the arrangement have passed their peak, why not allow them to air dry naturally in the container and keep on display a bit longer as a dried arrangement?

floral hurricane lamp

The magnificent array of colorful blooms and leaves that appear every autumn need not be limited to decorations for Halloween and Thanksgiving. Along with swags and garlands and hosts of other arrangements, leaf- and blossom-filled flowerpots can be placed around the house, quite simply, to celebrate the small but significant joys and blessings of every day, such as health, life, and love.

To add a warm glow and cheerful luster to our flowerpot, we've added a fat pillar candle and a hurricane lamp. As the candlelight washes over the petite wreath of flowers and fruit that surrounds the flowerpot, it seems to say: "Come on over, hang out with us, and be happy!" All are wishes we love to share with family and friends, no matter what the time of year. In this special sense of the term "to share," a wreath—be it mini, as pictured here, or magnanimous—is like a hug. Here the wreath encloses a candle. What will yours embrace?

floral hurricane lamp

Level of Difficulty: Easy

Time: ½ hour

Vase Life: Months

LEAVES, FLOWERS, AND BERRIES

2 stems preserved oak leaves (available from a craft shop—or to find out how to preserve your own, see Preserving Oak Leaves on page 197), 2 stems caspia, 2 stems solidago, 2 stems statice, 1 stem dried eucalyptus, 3 stems pepper berries

WHAT YOU NEED

- 8-inch-diameter terra-cotta flowerpot
- 2-inch-square piece of duct tape
- 2 pounds potting soil
- waterproof florist's tape
- 2 6-inch-long floral sticks
- 3- by 8-inch pillar candle
- sharp florist's scissors
- glue pan and glue pellets
- 8-inch-diameter grapevine wreath
- 3 clusters faux berries
- 5¼- by 14-inch hurricane lamp glass

FRESH **thoughts**®

Floral hurricane lamps look great in multiples. You can line a walkway with them, march them up either side of your front steps, or place several on your windowsill—or wherever you think you may want to add a "row of glow."

1 Cover the hole in the bottom of the flowerpot with duct tape and fill the flowerpot almost to the top with soil.

2 With waterproof florist's tape, tape the floral sticks to the pillar candle, one on either side. Insert the sticks into the dirt, pressing the base of the candle slightly into the soil until it is secure, so it will remain upright.

3 With the florist's scissors, cut the stems of all the flowers and leaves to 1- to 2-inch lengths.

4 Melt the glue pellets in the glue pan.

5 Dip the stem of an oak leaf into the hot glue. Insert the stem of the leaf through the strands of the grapevine wreath, and press the leaf against the grapevine to secure it. Repeat the process with all the leaves, inserting them at desired intervals around the wreath, checking to see that they will overlap the rim of the flowerpot when the wreath is placed on it.

Steps 1–2. Cover hole in flowerpot with duct tape; fill pot with soil. Tape floral sticks to pillar candle; stand candle in soil.

Steps 3–5. Cut stems of flowers and leaves to 2-inch lengths. Melt glue in glue pan. Dip oak-leaf stem in hot glue; insert stem in grapevine wreath; press to secure. Repeat for all leaves.

Steps 6–9. Repeat process for all flowers, mixing them, to fill wreath; add faux berries. Glue pepper berries to flowerpot. Place wreath on flowerpot.

6 Repeat the process for the caspia, solidago, statice, and dried eucalyptus, adding them one by one and mixing them up, until the wreath is as full as you like.

7 Glue the clusters of faux berries onto the wreath where desired.

8 Glue clusters of the pepper berries to the rim of the flowerpot, so they drape nicely.

9 Place the wreath on the rim of the flowerpot, on top of the pepper berries. Light the candle. Place the hurricane lamp over the candle, twisting it slightly to secure it in the bed of soil.

forever flowers

Drying flowers adds weeks, even months, to their vase life—and to your pleasure—especially if you want to preserve some flowers as a keepsake. That's why dried or preserved flowers are often called "everlastings." Air-drying is one way you can prolong the life of your flowers (for one method of air-drying, see our Floral Drying Rack on page 169). You can also preserve them by what's called the "moisture-transfer" method. Variations on this technique allow the blossoms to dry out in a desiccant, which may be an absorbent powder such as cornmeal, the laundry whitener known as Borax, or the granulated chemical compound craftspeople call silica gel. You can also have flowers freeze-dried by professionals who specialize in this service. This process is often requested by brides who want to keep their flowers looking precisely the way they did at their wedding.

The gorgeousness of this dried floral display belies the fact that the flowers are drying out at the same time as they are being admired. We've inserted leaves and mosses to cushion and frame each blossom or cluster of blooms. The colors and shapes of the flowers reflect the wide embrace of nature's bounty.

The technique you choose may be dictated by the flowers you want to preserve. Robust blooms with thick stems air-dry well. Flowers with fragile petals and "hollow" flowers, such as daffodils, should be dried in a desiccant. If you try to air-dry them, they will shrivel. Choose flowers at their peak. They should be completely dry, too, because dampness causes mold and petal discoloration. Preserve more flowers than you think you'll need for your arrangement. As they dry, some may become too brittle to handle.

You can use dried or preserved flowers in all kinds of arrangements, from garlands, swags, and wreaths to bouquets and contained arrangements such as the one on page 188. You can also press single petals within the pages of a journal or sew them into a pretty sachet.

air-drying

Many flowers can be air-dried; so can a number of herbs, grasses, and leaves. Plant matter that nature has preserved, such as pinecones, bark, desiccated twigs, stalks of wheat, cattails, and pieces of driftwood, add texture—and drama—to a display. There are four ways you can air-dry flowers.

- Suspended in small bunches of three to six blooms from nails or hooks attached to a ceiling beam
- String-tied, in small bunches, to a drying rack, as pictured on page 168
- Spread out individually on newspapers
- Stood upright, in a bunch with plenty of room to spare, in a vase, pail, or bucket.

Most craftspeople who air-dry flowers hang their blooms out of harm's way because the drying process can last anywhere from 10 days to a month—or more. If you decide to

stand your flowers upright in a container, make sure that all the blooms have plenty of air space around them. You can separate individual blossoms by enclosing them loosely in paper towels. Flowers dried individually on newspapers will have to be flipped halfway through the drying cycle; flipping ensures that the entire surface of each blossom is exposed to the air.

drying flowers in silica gel

Because of its astounding absorption rate, silica can dry a flower in 3 to 6 days—as opposed to air-drying, which can take a month or more. Using a microwave oven speeds up the process to mere minutes (see Using a Microwave Oven on page 193). Silica gel is expensive, but you can reuse it again and again. (To cut costs, mix silica, in equal parts, with Borax.) As silica absorbs moisture, it changes color from blue (or white) to pink. After use, bake silica in a standard oven set at 200 degrees F, until it returns to blue; when cool, store it in an airtight container until you need it again.

Flowers with fragile petals, such as anemones, pansies, violets, and peonies, and cuplike or hollow flowers, such as roses and tulips, should be dried face up. Heavier multi-petaled flowers, such as daisies or dahlias, can be dried face down (preferably in the microwave), while spiky flowers can be dried on their sides. After laying out your flowers and cutting back their stems to the desired length, fill a plastic container with a minimum 1-inch-deep bed of silica gel. (The rule of thumb is to pour in a depth equal to the length of the embedded stem, if any—

Flowers You Can Air-Dry with Success

baby's breath, delphinium, globe amaranth, globe artichoke, heather, hydrangea, larkspur, lavender, Queen Anne's lace, roses, solidago, statice, thistle, yarrow

Flowers That Dry Well in Desiccants

anemone, camellia, cosmos, dahlia, daisy, freesia, grape hyacinth, lilac, lily-of-the-valley, nasturtium, pansy, peony, ranunculus, rose

Flowers That Dry Well in Desiccants, in the Microwave

chrysanthemum, daisy, hydrangea, marigold, primrose, rose, zinnia

drying flowers in silica gel

plus 1 inch for the bed underneath.) Next, insert stems into the silica so that blossoms rest on top. They should not touch one another. Slowly spoon or sprinkle silica over the flowers, making sure you fill between every petal, until they are completely covered; pour an extra inch over the top.

Close the container and leave it in a warm place for 3 or 4 days. Check for dryness by lifting out one bloom. Don't let your flowers dry out too much, or they will become brittle and fall apart. When they are dry, remove them one by one with tweezers, and brush off the silica with a camel's hair paintbrush. (You can also remove silica using a hair dryer set at low. Blow silica into a bag; it can irritate your nose and throat if you accidentally inhale it.) If you are not going to arrange your flowers right away, you can store them for future use.

Using a Microwave Oven

Follow the instructions for drying flowers in silica gel, making sure the container you use is microwave safe. Set the microwave oven to low-to-medium power—between 4 and 5 on most standard models; on ovens with a temperature readout, the setting should be 350 degrees F. (A microwave with a turntable will be more efficient than one without; the rotation of the container enables flowers to dry evenly.)

One way to save a few flowers from a cherished gift or bouquet is to frame them. Choose a frame that appeals to you, and remove the glass. Using the glass as a template, cut a piece of paper or colored posterboard to fit the frame. After drying your blooms, hot-glue them onto the paper, along with the gift card sent by your beloved. Stand the frame on a mini-easel or frame it—where it can be seen and admired, of course!

After sealing the container, microwave it 3 minutes. Remove it, allow it to cool 15 minutes, and check the flowers for dryness. (Flowers will continue to "cook" for a few minutes.) If they still seem moist, zap them an additional 30 seconds. Cool them 15 minutes and check again.

What You Need to Dry Flowers in Desiccant

- box with a tight lid, such as plastic food storage container
- sharp florist's scissors, to cut flowers
- tweezers, to remove blooms from desiccant
- narrow camel's hair paintbrush, to brush off desiccant
- painter's respirator mask, to prevent nose and throat irritation

–Lisa Aliment
Redmond, WA

drying flowers in Borax or cornmeal

The laundry brightener Borax has been a household staple for decades. Like silica gel, Borax (and cornmeal) absorb moisture from flowers, but it takes longer—at least a week or more to dry flowers thoroughly. Borax and cornmeal are nontoxic and inexpensive. You can mix them with each other, or Borax with silica gel, in equal parts. Follow the instructions for Drying Flowers in Silica Gel on page 191, making sure you cover the flowers completely. Seal the container and leave it in a warm, dry place. Check for dryness after a week. Like silica, Borax, used alone, can be recycled. Cornmeal, however, does not last indefinitely.

storing dried flowers

No matter how and where you display them, all dried flowers begin to fade after a few weeks. If you like, you can save dried flowers or an arrangement made with them to bring out at a later date. (Don't store them in plastic, though; they need air to "breathe," even in storage.) Lay several sheets of tissue or waxed paper in the bottom of a cardboard box, such as a shoebox. Crumple several more sheets and twist them into loose rolls; rest the rolls of paper in the box. Place the dried flowers (or arrangement) in the box, without crowding, using the paper rolls to support the flowers at their necks, right under the flowerheads. Close the box and place it in a cool, dry place.

FRESH thoughts®

Freeze-Drying Flowers

Freeze-drying is a specialized technique for preserving flowers that can only be done by pros who have the heavy-duty equipment that can handle the job. Even though freeze-drying is an expensive way to dry flowers—it costs between $1 and $5 per stem—it is popular because the technique allows fresh flowers to be saved indefinitely in their "truest" and most colorful state, without wilting. Many people choose this method to preserve very important flowers, such as wedding bouquets. The flowers are treated with a starch that "sets" the color and then frozen in a specially designed vacuum chamber.

You can sew—or tie—dried scented flowers into lovely little sachets. One of our favorite sachet-fillers is lavender, which is said to ward off moths. If you want to see the flower filler after it has been sewn up, use organza; otherwise, any fabric swatches or snippets will do. Besides placing them in your sweater drawers, why not tuck pairs of sachets in your shoes, too? They are perfect "odor-eaters"!

wiring stems and flowers

Drying and preserving flowers is harsh on stems, causing them to become brittle and break. No matter! You can replace or reinforce stems with wire—but only if you do not microwave them. (You can't put metal in microwaves.) Florists and nurseries stock an array of florist's wire in various thicknesses, or gauges, and in two lengths: 1 foot and 18 inches. Medium-gauge wire is the one used most because it is strong and flexible enough to secure most stems. Thin spool wire is often used for flowers with delicate stems.

Flowers can be wired in one of four ways:

- by coiling the wire around the stem
- by snipping off most of the stem and winding fine-gauge wire around it and a piece of heavier wire to create a new "stem"
- by threading the wire up through a hollow stem
- by wiring the flower from the top. To do this, make a hairpin bend at one end of the wire, insert it into the flowerhead, and push it through until the hairpin catches; coil the remainder of the wire around the stem.

When you wire a flower, use a piece that's at least twice as long as the stem to give you enough to make the requisite twists; you can cut off excess later. The most common mistake is to overwire. Usually a twist or two (or three) is enough. Once you've wired your stem, wind florist's tape around it to secure and hide the wire.

wiring fruit

Because of their weight, fruit, such as the apples pictured on our Harvest Garland on page 161, must be wired individually and separately from lighter-weight flowers and leaves. Nothing could be simpler.

Using 12-inch-long (or 18-inch-long) fine-gauge florist's wire, cut two pieces of wire with wire cutters for each piece of fruit. The length of the wire you use and each piece of wire you cut will be dictated by the size of the fruit. Triple the diameter of the fruit, so you can twist the ends of the wire together at the base of the fruit and still have enough wire left over to attach the fruit to the display. Pierce the fruit—at the spot that it will be inserted into the display—with one piece of wire and push it through, centering the fruit on the wire. Repeat the process with the second piece of wire, inserting it at right angles to the first one. With needle-nosed pliers, bend the ends of the wires until they meet at the base of the fruit. Twist the ends together.

As you set about creating any arrangement that contains fruit, keep in mind how and where you want to display your fruit on the arrangement. Do you want to cluster your fruit, or would you prefer to distribute individual pieces of fruit throughout the display? Which side of a particular piece of fruit do you want to face outward? Do you want its stem to show, and, if so, which direction do you want it to point? Do you want to display different fruits from different angles? After making your decision, wire the fruit on the opposite side from the side that will show its face.

bloomnet®
basics

Preserving Oak Leaves

If you'd like to preserve oak leaves that you've picked up on your autumn strolls for several of our Fall projects rather than purchase them at a craft store, it's easy to do so. You just soak them in a solution of water and glycerine and allow them to dry completely, a process that takes about 2 weeks. (You can pick up glycerine at a craft shop or pharmacy.) Leaves need plenty of room to rest in the preservative solution, so use a large, shallow baking pan or lasagna dish.

To make the solution, mix 1 part glycerine to 2 parts hot water, then pour it into your pan. Drop the leaves into the solution, and let them soak for 4 days. Next, remove the leaves and lay them out on paper towels. After a couple of days, cover them with more paper towels and place some heavy books on top to prevent the leaves from curling up at their edges. Allow them to rest under the weight for 10 more days. Preserved oak leaves should keep for months.

–Gayla Blackwell
Vine Grove, KY

winter

winter
thoughts

Most people think of winter as the season when the earth lies dormant and plants go into hiding. But that's not true. Nature may look like she's taking a break—but she's not; nor are we! Look at all the wonderful evergreens that lend softness to the muted landscape around you. Look at the clusters of berries peeping out from under a crystalline veil of snow.

For most of us, winter is a season of celebration, of holidays both religious and secular, which warm our hearts and sing to our souls. Even before the last of the turkey has been consumed, thoughts turn to Christmas, Hanukkah, and Kwanzaa. For some people, in fact, decorating for the holidays starts even before Thanksgiving.

So, what are we going to do about decorating the house this year? Some of the things we do are time-honored family traditions, like figuring out whose stocking goes where on the mantel or which ornaments will decorate the wreath on the front door. But this season is also a time to indulge your imagination, to see what new and wonderful decorations you can dream up.

To inspire you, we're offering you some of our favorite holiday projects, plus some other easy ideas that we hope will send you on some fabulous flight of fancy.

Later, after the hullabaloo of the holidays is over, isn't it wonderful to relax and enjoy a cup of cocoa by the fire or curl up with a good book—or DVD? We think so, especially after a walk in the crunchy snow. After all, we have one winter holiday to go: Valentine's Day. This one's our all-time favorite, and we say it with roses—with millions and millions of them, in fact! What a great way to end a season and begin a new flower-filled year.

potpourri vase

Filling a Potpourri Vase is fun! For dramatic effect, we took some prepackaged potpourri that we found at our local craft shop, mixed it together with some dried roses and pinecones, then poured it all over a bed of green pine needles—but you can drop in any dried flowers and plant matter that will hold its shape, such as dried bark or moss. (For dried flowers that would look colorful in a potpourri vase, turn to the Fall Seasonal Specialty on page 189.)

The trick to making a potpourri vase is that it comes in two parts: The first is a wide-mouthed bubble bowl or fish bowl; the second is a narrow drinking glass that's the same height as the bowl. The space between them becomes the enclosure for your dried material, while the glass holds water so you can enjoy some seasonal fresh flowers when you complete your display. We chose tulips and flowering hypericum, but you could use any flowers you find at the florist. Just make sure they'll fit in your glass.

potpourri vase

tulip

hypericum

Level of Difficulty: Easy

Time: 20 minutes

Vase Life: Fresh flowers, 1 week

Dried roses, pine, and pinecones, several weeks

FLOWERS

15 tulips, 7 flowering hypericum

WHAT YOU NEED

■ sprigs of pine

■ 10-inch-wide by 10½-inch-high bubble bowl or
fish bowl (with a 7-inch-diameter opening)

■ 1 large bag (approximately 22 ounces) potpourri,
available at a craft shop

■ 6 small pinecones

■ 10½-inch-high drinking glass (The glass must be as high
as or slightly higher than the bowl you are using and
must be narrower than its opening.)

■ sharp florist's scissors

Quick tip

The easiest way to move
large, individual elements,
such as pinecones and
roses, around in the
potpourri is to use the
handle of a long wooden
kitchen spoon.

1 Place the sprigs of pine at the bottom of the bubble bowl or fish bowl, if desired. Fill the bubble bowl half full with prepackaged potpourri mix. Add the pinecones (and a couple of dried roses and snapdragon, if desired), twisting them into the mixture so that that they are visible through the sides of the bowl.

2 Insert the glass into the bowl, twisting it through the potpourri mixture until it hits the bottom of the bowl. Once the glass is in place, fill the space between the glass and the bowl with the remainder of the packaged potpourri. (If the space between is very narrow, you can use a narrow funnel to direct the flow of potpourri.)

3 Fill the glass one-third full with water. With florist's scissors, cut the stems of the tulips and hypericum and arrange them in the glass.

Step 1. Place bed of pine at bottom of bowl (or fill bowl full with packaged potpourri mix) followed by pinecones and dried roses.

Step 2. Insert glass in bowl, twisting it until it hits bottom of bowl. Fill space between glass and bowl with remaining flowers or potpourri mix.

Step 3. Fill glass ¹/₃ full with water. Cut tulips and hypericum and arrange in glass.

FRESH thoughts®

If you are creating your potpourri vase for the holidays, be on the lookout for seasonal greens and berries to enhance your arrangement. You can also add fake berries and miniature fake fruits, such as lady apples and gilded pears, to the mix—or even miniature Christmas tree balls. Craft and hobby shops and mega-stores are full of baubles and bangles and beads at this time of year, as well as other holiday craft supplies.

Here's a list of "extras" we added to our potpourri vase to give it some zing:

- 4 sprigs of pine
- 8 dried roses
- 1 dried snapdragon
- small handful of spanish moss

mantel
garland

In many an American home, the fireplace is the primary focus of a holiday decorating scheme. Here stockings are hung, stories are read—and cookies and milk set out to stave off Santa's hunger as he makes his yearly rounds. The Christmas tree stands nearby. One of the most festive color schemes for the holiday season, pictured here, is green and white with gold; depending on which of the seasonal holidays you celebrate, you can substitute silver for the gold or offset the white with blue. Or, if you prefer, you can stick with traditional red (for more red ideas, turn to Who Needs Ornaments? on page 251).

A mantelpiece ledge provides an especially attractive venue to showcase a welcoming holiday garland. Our mantel is five feet long, so we had to use four bricks of floral foam for our display; once you've measured your own mantel, you can measure and cut your bricks of floral foam so that they will fit. We used lots of different kinds of white flowers for our garland, but you could use fewer varieties—or only one. It's up to you!

mantel garland

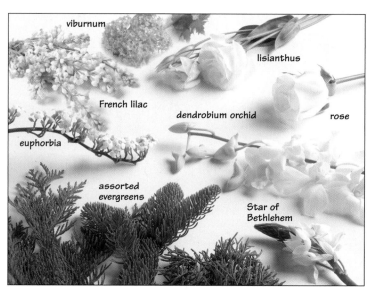

viburnum

French lilac

lisianthus

dendrobium orchid

rose

euphorbia

assorted evergreens

Star of Bethlehem

Level of Difficulty: Difficult

Time: 1½ hours

Vase Life: 1 to 2 weeks

GREENS, FLOWERS, FRUIT, AND VEGETABLES

3 branches assorted evergreens (such as cedar, pine, juniper, balsam), 5 Star of Bethlehem, 10 stems dendrobium orchids, 10 stems euphorbia, 10 French lilac, 10 roses, 5 viburnum, 5 lisianthus, 5 small clusters green grapes, 2 artichokes

WHAT YOU NEED

- 4 bricks floral foam
- 4 11- by 6-inch waterproof trays or plastic liners
- green waterproof florist's tape
- 39 6-inch-long floral sticks
- 4 9-inch-tall pillar candles and 6 6-inch-tall pillar candles
- pruning shears
- sharp florist's scissors
- 15 12-inch-long pieces medium-gauge florist's wire
- 4 gold Styrofoam apples
- 1¼-inch-wide gold, wired ribbon (5 strips 18-inches long; 5 strips 12-inches long)
- sharp paring knife
- grapefruit spoon
- 2 votive candles

bloomnet®
basics

To keep your garland looking fresh, remove individual blossoms as they pass their blooming time and replace them with new flowers, as desired. The greens should last up to 3 weeks; you may want to switch to an all-green display as time goes on.

—Jay Casiano
New York, NY

1 Place the floral foam in the trays. Cut pieces of florist's tape and crisscross them around and over the floral foam to secure each brick to its tray. Soak the floral-foam-filled trays in water.

2 With florist's tape, secure 2 floral sticks to each pillar candle.

3 Insert the pillar candles into the floral foam, clustering them, as you desire. Once the floral sticks are in position, press the candles slightly into the floral foam for extra stability.

4 With the pruning shears, cut the evergreens to a length that will drape a few inches over the fronts of the trays (and slightly over the edge of the mantelpiece). Insert the evergreens into the floral foam, until you have built up a waterfall-like bed of greens around the candles.

5 Separate the flowers by variety. With the florist's scissors, cut the stems of the flowers one by one, and insert them one by one into the floral foam, as desired, to fill the gaps between the evergreens.

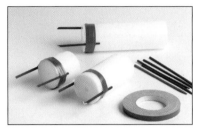

Step 1. Place floral foam in trays; crisscross florist's tape over foam to secure to trays. Saturate with water.

Steps 2–3. Tape 2 floral sticks to each pillar candle; insert sticks holding candles in foam (not shown).

Step 4. Prune evergreens to lengths that will drape over front of tray and mantel. Insert greens into floral foam to build up bed around candles.

Step 5. Cut stems of flowers; separate by variety. Insert flowers one by one in arrangement to fill gaps between greens.

Step 8. Fold a strip of ribbon in half and wire it to the end of a floral stick.

6 Bend five pieces of medium-gauge wire into U-shaped hairpins. Twist a U-shaped wire around the stem of a grape cluster, and twist the ends of the wire around a floral stick. Insert the floral stick holding the grapes into the floral foam where desired. Repeat the process for the remaining grape clusters.

7 Insert a floral stick into the bottom of each of the Styrofoam apples, and insert the apples into the arrangement where desired.

8 Fold a strip of ribbon in half to create a loop, and wire it to the end of a floral stick. Repeat the process for all 10 ribbon strips (5 short and 5 long). Insert the longer loops near the bottom of the arrangement and the shorter ones near the top.

9 Hollow out an artichoke per the instructions for Nature's Place Card on page 67. Repeat with the other artichoke. Fill the hollows of the artichokes with votive candles. Place the artichoke votives at either end of the mantelpiece or where desired.

winter window box

I t is virtually impossible to go wrong when mixing winter's greens. Nature, after all, does this all the time, allowing conifers, hollies, yews, and other evergreens to commingle in her forests. With periodic misting and watering, branches, twigs, and sprigs of green will keep for weeks, whether they're arranged in an interior window box, as pictured here, or in another container of your choosing. For color, we've added holly berry, but you can insert bittersweet, pepper berry, or another colorful berry instead. During the holidays—or all season long—an electric candle twinkles through the window at passersby.

Outdoor window boxes can be filled and decorated the same way as interior ones are; the only thing you need to remember is to use weatherproof containers. Garden centers and nurseries usually keep these in good supply; choose ones that will show off and complement your arrangements.

winter window box

Level of Difficulty: Easy

Time: ½ hour

Vase Life: 2 to 3 weeks

GREENS AND BERRIES

3 branches balsam, 3 branches cedar, 3 branches Western cedar, 6 branches white pine, 6 branches holly with berries, 2 branches juniper with berries

WHAT YOU NEED

■ 9-inch-high by 30-inch-long by 8-inch-deep window box

■ plastic liner or heavy-duty plastic garbage bag, if necessary

■ 3 bricks floral foam

■ electric candle (optional) and extension cord, if necessary

■ pruning shears

Quick tip

Some window boxes come with liners; check your home or garden center to see if they carry window boxes with prefitted inserts. Some styles are constructed of molded plastic so they don't require liners at all.

1 Assuming your window box is not watertight, cut the plastic liner or garbage bag to fit the box. Fold under the edges of the liner to hide them.

2 Soak the floral foam thoroughly in water and place the wet floral foam in the liner.

3 (optional): If you are going to accent your arrangement with an electric candle, center it on the floral foam at this stage of your project and press the base of the candle into the floral foam to stabilize it.

4 With the pruning shears, cut the greens one by one to a length that will allow each branch to drape 6 inches over the rim of the window box (lengths will vary according to where individual greens are placed in the box).

5 Insert the greens into the floral foam one by one, as desired, creating a bed around the electric candle.

6 Cut and insert sprigs of the holly with berries, where desired.

Step 1. Cut plastic liner to fit window box. Position liner in box; fold edges under to hide them.

Steps 2–3. Place water-soaked floral foam in lined box. Center electric candle on foam; press candle into foam to stabilize it.

Steps 4–6. Prune evergreens to lengths that will drape over rim of box; insert greens, as desired, in foam. Cut sprigs of holly; insert in foam to fill gaps.

bloomnet®
basics

If you live in the country, you can make a special foray into the woods with pruning shears to lop off branches from the various evergreens you find there, and collect them to use in your seasonal displays. In the suburbs, you can do some judicious pruning of evergreens in your yard. Otherwise, you'll have to take advantage of what's for sale at your local nursery or florist.

One way to collect a mass of a single kind of evergreen is from your Christmas tree. Lop off the bottom branches as raw material for your arrangements, and then saw back the trunk of the tree to the size that will fit your tree stand—and your room.

–Joanna Zeruos
Bethel Park, PA

kissing ball

Custom has it that mistletoe symbolizes peace and goodwill. In ancient Greece, enemies who happened to meet under a tree overgrown with mistletoe immediately declared a truce. In early Anglo-Saxon England, exchanging kisses under mistletoe suspended from the ceiling was a sign of friendship. To celebrate the Twelve Days of Christmas, looped garlands of evergreens called kissing boughs were accented with candles and mistletoe to decorate homes— and all this occurred long before the advent of the Christmas tree!

Our Kissing Ball takes its cue from the evergreen bough, so it can be enjoyed throughout the holiday season. We suspended the floral-foam form in our doorway and then proceeded with our project, adding our mistletoe and ribbon at the last minute. If you go this route, you may need a helper to snip the pieces of boxwood and hand them up to you as you work. Remember that the wet floral foam may drip, so it's a good idea to lay a piece of plastic underneath to protect the floor.

kissing ball

boxwood

white pine

mistletoe

holly

Western cedar

juniper

Level of Difficulty: Moderate
Time: 45 minutes
Vase Life: 2 to 3 weeks

EVERGREENS AND MISTLETOE

$^1/_2$ pound boxwood, 1 branch juniper with berries,
1 branch Western cedar, 1 branch holly, 1 branch white pine,
1 to 2 bags preserved mistletoe (or fake mistletoe)

WHAT YOU NEED

- $^1/_2$ brick floral foam
- 13- by 12-inch piece chicken wire
- 12 inches red cord
- step stool
- 1 cup hook
- pruning shears
- 1 12-inch-long piece medium-gauge florist's wire
- 1 yard red ribbon
- 1 12-inch-long piece fine-gauge florist's wire
- sharp household or craft scissors

Quick tip

Another easy way to do the project is to perch the form on top of a vase and work at your kitchen table—and then hang it after it is complete.

1 Soak the floral foam in water.

2 Wrap the chicken wire around the wet floral foam to create a cage, turning the exposed edges of the chicken wire into the floral foam to conceal them.

3 Tie the cord to the top of the chicken-wire–wrapped form. Tie a loop at the opposite end of the cord.

4 Standing on the step stool, center the cup hook on top of the trim at the top of your chosen doorway. Screw in the cup hook to secure it, and hang the kissing-ball form from the cup hook.

5 With the pruning shears, snip the boxwood into small pieces, leaving 2 to 4 inches of stem on each. Insert the boxwood stems, as desired, through the chicken wire into the floral foam until you achieve a nice, full ball shape.

Steps 1–3: Wrap wet floral foam in chicken wire. Tie cord to form and tie loop at other end of cord.

Step 5. Insert snips of boxwood into floral foam to create ball shape.

Steps 6–7. Prune remaining greens; insert in ball. Wire mistletoe and insert in bottom of ball.

Step 8. Tie and wire ribbon bow and insert in bottom of ball.

6 Cut the remaining greens— we used juniper with its berries, Western cedar, holly with its berries, and white pine— into 4-inch-long pieces. Using the greens as accent pieces, insert them throughout the ball of boxwood, as desired.

7 Fold the piece of medium-gauge florist's wire in half. Center the mistletoe on the wire and wrap the wire around the mistletoe stems, twisting the ends of the wire together. Insert the wires into the bottom of the kissing ball, making sure that the mistletoe hangs lower than the bottom-most greens in the ball.

8 Using the red ribbon, tie a decorative floral bow. Wind the piece of fine-gauge florist's wire around the center of the bow; insert the wired ribbon into the base of the ball, next to the mistletoe. With scissors, cut the ends of the ribbon into V-shaped swallowtails, if desired.

9 KISS!

pear place card

One of the tricks of setting a beautiful table is to find a theme for your party or other occasion. The theme may celebrate an event, such as a birthday, or it may celebrate a season—in this case, Winter. As pictured here, the entire table is decorated with pillar candles and miniature bottles so that it becomes both invitation and display. Each bottle holds a single bloom or spray of white flowers to complete our green-and-white theme.

At each place setting, a saucer displays a sprig of cedar and a pinecone—and a pear that's been slit to accept a place card. Pears abound during the winter months; look for a firm, upright variety that can stand on its end without tipping over. Once each guest finds his or her place at the table, the place plate can be removed and the first course served on the larger plate beneath.

pear place card

pinecone

dendrobium orchid

Western cedar

Level of Difficulty: Easy
Time: 20 minutes per pear
Vase Life: 1 day

FRUIT, GREENS, AND PINECONES

1 branch Western cedar (should supply enough greens for all place cards and plates), 1 firm, hard, upright pear per guest, 1 or 2 stems dendrobium orchid (each stem bears 8 blooms, and you'll need one bloom per place card), 1 pinecone per plate

WHAT YOU NEED

■ pruning shears

■ 1 dessert plate per guest

■ 2- by 3-inch place card, or plain card, per guest

■ single-edge razor blade, or artist's matte knife

■ glue pan and glue pellets

■ sharp florist's scissors

■ paring knife

FRESH thoughts®

Using white flowers with evergreens—plus natural touches such as pinecones—creates a look that is casual and elegant at the same time.

To extend the theme, place a selection of white blooms in little bottles or vases, and scatter them over the table with pillar candles between them.

1 With the pruning shears, cut 4-inch-long sprigs of Western cedar to place on all the dessert plates. Place one 4-inch-long sprig on the center of each plate. Cut a 2-inch-long snip of cedar for each of the place cards; set them aside.

2 Prepare a place card, as shown, with the name of a guest. With the razor blade or matte knife, cut two slits in one corner of the place card. Insert a 2-inch snip of cedar between the slits.

3 Melt the glue pellets in the glue pan.

4 With the florist's scissors, snip the dendrobium orchid blossoms off their stem, one for each pear.

5 Dip the underside of an orchid blossom into the glue pan, and glue the blossom to the top of a pear.

6 With the paring knife, make an incision in the pear. Insert the place card in the incision, and place the pear on the cedar on the plate.

7 Place a pinecone next to the pear on the plate. Repeat Steps 1 through 7 for each guest.

Steps 3–5. Melt glue in glue pan. Snip dendrobium blossom off spike; hot-glue bottom of blossom to top of pear.

Step 6. Make incision in pear. Insert place card in incision.

Quick tip

Winter pears come in a wide variety of shapes and textures. Choose the type—and color—that coordinates best with your table setting.

If a green scheme and pears just won't do for your particular occasion, you can use apples instead, which range from pale Yellow Delicious to deep red Rome and McIntosh. Some varieties, like Gala, are striated, which can look very pretty in a table setting.

kids' play vases

During the long winter months, Mom and Dad look for ways to occupy the kids with indoor activities. What better way to spend some free time between and after the holidays than doing a great project together that's pretty, too. Choosing flowers, cutting their stems, and arranging them in a vase is easy, even for little fingers. And, making special containers for the flower arrangements is also lots of fun.

The projects pictured here—the Crayon Vase and the Lego® Vase—are two examples of what you can do with kids. Both start with a can (or a jelly jar) and a brick of floral foam; you and the kids take it from there. The only thing you'll have to remember is to choose a can that can be completely concealed by the crayons, with their tips showing at the top, like a crown. And, remember: At any time of the year, these little vases make great gifts for Grandma—or for a favorite teacher. Almost any flowers will work in either container as long as they have smallish blossoms.

kids' play vases

CRAYON VASE

LEGO® VASE

Level of Difficulty: Easy

Time: 20 minutes per vase

Vase Life: 7 to 10 days

FLOWERS, FOR THE CRAYON VASE

1 lily, 1 stem mini-carnation, 1 stem daisy pom, 1 stem solidago, 1 stem statice

WHAT YOU NEED FOR THE CRAYON VASE

- ⅓ brick floral foam
- approximately 3½-inch-high by 4-inch-diameter can, or other small watertight container
- rubber band, big enough to fit around can
- 36 crayons
- florist's scissors or household scissors
- 6 pipe cleaners, in a variety of colors

FLOWERS, FOR THE LEGO® VASE

2 stems solidago, 2 stems statice, 3 sunflowers, 4 carnations

WHAT YOU NEED FOR THE LEGO® VASE

- ⅙ brick floral foam
- 4-inch-square by 3-inch-high condiment dish, or other small watertight container
- approximately 60 Legos®, in varying colors and sizes

Crayon Vase

1 Soak the floral foam in water, and place the wet floral foam in the can or container.

2 Place the rubber band around the can, midway up the can.

3 Insert the crayons behind the rubber band, one by one, until they cover the can.

4 With the scissors, cut the stems of all the flowers for your child. The stems should be 4 to 7 inches long.

5 Insert the flowers, as desired, into the floral foam, placing the tallest ones at the center and fanning out from there. Here, the tallest—and biggest—flower is a lily.

6 Twist two pipe cleaners together; wrap the twisted pipe cleaners around the rubber band. Curl the ends of the pipe cleaners into coils or into any desired shape. Repeat the process with two more pipe cleaners. Add the last two pipe cleaners around the tied ends, as pictured in main photo, to make a "floral bow."

Steps 1–2, for both vases; Step 3 for Crayon Vase: Cut and place water-soaked floral foam in containers. Build walls around containers— Crayons behind rubber band placed around can, Legos around dish.

Step 3 for Lego Vase; Steps 4–5 for Crayon Vase: Cut flowers to desired lengths; insert in floral foam in both containers.

Step 6 for Crayon Vase: Twist two pipe cleaners together; wrap around vase to hide rubber band. Curl ends of pipe cleaners into coils.

Lego® Vase

1 Follow Step 1 as outlined for the Crayon Vase.

2 Build walls of Lego® blocks around the container. Keep adding Legos® until the sides of the container are covered. Note: If you want to transport your Lego® vase, it will have to sit on a small saucer or plate because it has no bottom.

3 Follow Steps 4 and 5, as outlined opposite, for the Crayon Vase. Here, the carnation is the tallest flower.

victorian flower wreath

The popularity of wreaths is nothing short of wonderful—not only at Christmas, but also throughout the year. During the holidays, we especially enjoy evergreen wreaths. Their aroma is delicious, and the way they look on a front door or in the windows, whether they are decorated to the nines or accented only with a fat red bow, seems utterly magical when the air is nippy and the ground covered in snow. We also love to make wreaths that feature fresh flowers along with the greens and then display them indoors. Victorian Flower Wreaths are a beautiful way, for instance, to dress up the inside of French doors.

The best types of flowers to use are those that will also air-dry well (see our list of candidates in Flowers You Can Air-Dry with Success on page 191), because then they'll outlast the holiday season. Add some of your most cherished ornaments, too, if you like, and your wreath will proclaim that you are ready to extend a welcome to one and all—even into the New Year.

victorian flower wreath

waxflower

caspia

statice

baby's breath

rose

heather

Level of Difficulty: Easy
Time: ½ hour
Vase Life: 3 weeks or more

FLOWERS

6 roses, 1 stem baby's breath, 2 stems caspia,
4 stems heather, 2 stems statice, 2 stems waxflower

WHAT YOU NEED

- sharp craft or household scissors
- 3 yards red ribbon of your choice
- 20-inch-diameter evergreen wreath
- 3 12-inch-long pieces fine-gauge florist's wire, cut in half
- hot glue pan and glue pellets
- sharp florist's scissors
- green floral stem wrap

Quick tip

What is wonderful about this project is that you can start off with any evergreen wreath you choose. You might want to prune it so it's shape is neat and round. Just make sure it's unadorned, because decorating it will be the fun part!

1 With the sharp craft scissors, cut 3 yards of ribbon. Using the ribbon, make a floral bow at the center of the ribbon, per our Bloomnet® Basics on page 41. Using the wire that secures the center of the bow, attach the bow to the top of the wreath, allowing the long ends of the ribbon to hang free.

2 Lace the long ends of the ribbon through the wreath. Secure the ribbon to the evergreens, where desired, with the pieces of florist's wire.

3 Heat the glue pellets in the glue pan.

4 With the florist's scissors, cut the stems of the roses to 2-inch lengths. Dip the stem and back of a rose in hot glue and attach it to the wreath where desired. Repeat with all the roses, positioning them at intervals around the wreath.

Steps 1–2. Make bow at center of a 3-yard-long piece of ribbon; attach to top of wreath. Lace 2 long ends of ribbon through wreath, attaching them with wire here and there to secure to wreath. Cut off excess.

Steps 4–6. Cut roses to 2-inch lengths; hot-glue to wreath. Cut stems of remaining flowers to same length; secure clusters of stems, by flower type, with stem wrap. Hot-glue clusters to wreath where desired.

5 Cut the stems of the remaining flowers—baby's breath, caspia, heather, statice, and waxflower—to 2-inch lengths. Cluster several blossoms of each type of flower and secure their stems with stem wrap. Repeat with all the flowers.

6 Dip the stems of one cluster of flowers in hot glue and attach it to the wreath where desired. Repeat with the remaining clusters until the wreath is as full as you like, making sure to attach some where the ribbon is wired, to hide the wires.

FRESH thoughts®

To ensure that your wreath will last as long as possible, don't place it near a source of heat such as a radiator. Mist it every other day to keep it fresh.

good fortune bouquet™

Americans are lucky. We live in such a cosmopolitan nation that most of us—particularly those of us who live in metropolitan areas—can sample ethnic cuisines from many different countries from around the world. By far the most popular style of cooking, especially in big cities like New York, where my family comes from, is what we've come to call "Chinese"—as in "Chinese take-out" or "Anyone up for Chinese?" We love the idea of everyone choosing a dish and then having everyone share what is set out on the table. We also love the containers that Chinese food comes in.

One day, we realized: Wow! These would make wonderful containers for flowers, too! The only thing you have to be careful of is whether the container is watertight or not; to be on the safe side, you can line it with plastic before inserting the water-saturated floral foam; a plastic sandwich bag works well for this purpose. Better be safe than sorry.

good fortune bouquet™

rose

hypericum

Level of Difficulty: Easy
Time: 20 minutes
Vase Life: 1 week or more

FLOWERS

6 roses, 4 stems hypericum

WHAT YOU NEED

- ½ brick floral foam
- 1 quart-size, clean Chinese take-out container
- sharp florist's scissors
- 2 chopsticks
- 12-inch-long piece of raffia
- 1 6-inch-long floral stick
- 1 fortune cookie

Quick tip

For a dinner party, use larger take-out containers as table decorations and the smallest-size ones as place-card holders. Write the names of your guests on tiny strips of paper, and insert one in the free end of each fortune cookie—like a fortune. Insert the fortune cookie in each small container (see Step 4 on opposite page). Your guests will feel lucky indeed!

1 Soak the floral foam in water. Place the wet floral foam in the Chinese-food container.

2 With the florist's scissors, cut the stems of the roses and hypericum to 2-inch lengths, and insert them as you cut them, one by one, into the floral foam, keeping the arrangement low and tightly clustered.

3 Tie the chopsticks together with raffia, and tie them to the handle of the container.

4 Insert the floral stick into one end of the fortune cookie. Position the fortune cookie between two flowers, and insert the stick into the floral foam to secure the cookie.

Step 1. Place water-soaked floral foam in Chinese-food container.

Step 2. Cut stems of roses and hypericum to 2-inch lengths; insert flowers in floral foam, clustering them tightly.

Steps 3–4. Tie chopsticks, with raffia, to container. Insert floral stick in fortune cookie; add cookie to arrangement (not shown).

FRESH thoughts®

Red is such a delicious color, and, to the Chinese, it means good luck, too. There are lots of wonderful red flowers you can use in your bouquet. Here are just a few of the most common ones, all available in red, naturally!

- carnation
- chrysanthemum
- cockscomb
- dahlia
- gerbera daisy
- lily
- tulip
- zinnia

Even though red is a good-luck color, that doesn't mean that you are obligated to create a red bouquet in your take-out container. Indeed, you can make yours with any flowers—in any single color or mix of colors—that work for you. The only thing to take into account is the size and shape of the blossoms. You want to be sure they will not be so top-heavy that they'll cause the container to topple over!

holiday flower tree®

This is one of the very first signature arrangements introduced by our company, and it continues to be one of the most popular arrangements we offer every holiday season. Each year, we come out with a different variation. The Holiday Flower Tree® we're offering you here is one of our favorites. It's based on the famous Christmas carol entitled "A Partridge in a Pear Tree."

The wonderful thing about holiday flower trees is that they can be created in virtually any size you want, from a tiny, few inches to a generous foot or two—or more. Obviously, you can cover your tree with any flowers you like, too. We chose miniature carnations as the featured flower and complemented them with Star of Bethlehem and statice—plus fake gold pears. The green is boxwood, which features lovely shiny small leaves that are perfectly in scale with the size of the holiday tree. You could also use any small-needled pine or another holiday green such as holly. It's up to you!

holiday flower tree®

statice

Star of
Bethlehem

mini-carnation

boxwood

Level of Difficulty: Moderate

Time: 1 hour

Vase Life: 2 to 3 weeks, with daily misting

FLOWERS AND GREENS

approximately ³/₄ pound boxwood, 3 stems mini-carnation
(approximately 12 flowers), 3 stems statice, 9 Star of Bethlehem

WHAT YOU NEED

- 1 brick floral foam
- 6-inch shallow waterproof dish
- sharp florist's, craft, or household scissors
- waterproof florist's tape
- pruning shears or clippers
- 12 6-inch-long floral sticks
- 12 miniature gold Styrofoam pears
- 12-inch-long piece medium-gauge florist's wire, cut in half
- partridge-in-nest ornament, available from a craft or hobby shop

Quick tip

Boxwood comes in multi-branched pieces; break it into smaller and smaller pieces as you go along. Or, break it up into pieces of various lengths ahead of time, and pluck the size you need from the pile.

1 Place the floral foam in the dish. Cut and crisscross two pieces of florist's tape around and over the floral foam to secure the brick to the dish. Soak the floral-foam–filled dish in water.

2 With the pruning shears or clippers, cut a straight, pointy sprig of boxwood for the top of the tree to the length you want to establish as the desired height of your tree. Insert the boxwood sprig into the top of the floral foam.

3 Cut four sprigs of boxwood to the length you want to establish as the width of your tree, and insert them into the base of the floral foam on all four sides. Remember that you'll want the base of your tree to conceal the rim of the dish.

4 Continue cutting sprigs of boxwood, and insert them at strategic points on every side of the floral foam, making sure they are the correct length so that the sides of the tree will taper from top to bottom.

5 Turning the dish, fill in the gaps with sprigs of boxwood until the tree is completely "leafed out" and assumes its traditional conical shape.

Step 1. Place floral foam in dish; secure with crisscrossed florist's tape.

Steps 2–5. Insert one pointy sprig of boxwood at top of foam. Add four sprigs at base of foam. Add sprigs at different lengths to create conical tree shape.

Steps 6–8. Cut stems of flowers to 2-inch lengths; insert into boxwood. Insert floral sticks into mini-pears; insert into tree.

Step 9. Thread wire through back of partridge's nest; twist ends of wire. Insert wired nest to tree.

6 With the scissors, cut the blossoms of the mini-carnations from their stems, leaving 2-inch-long stems below the blossoms. Insert them in the tree where desired.

7 Cut 2-inch-long sprigs of the statice, and insert them into the tree where desired. Repeat the process with the Star of Bethlehem.

8 Insert a floral stick into the side of a miniature pear at its base. Repeat this with all the pears. Insert the pears into the tree wherever desired, spacing them around the entire tree.

9 Using a 6-inch-long piece of florist's wire, insert it through the back of the partridge's nest and twist the ends of the wire together. Insert the wires into the floral foam to wire the nest to the tree.

holiday
snowman

Inspired by the popularity of our annual Holiday Flower Tree®
(see page 237), we put our heads together to figure out some other
designs that would be as much fun to give or receive—and equally
easy to make. One of the ideas we came up with is this chipper little
Holiday Snowman. In winter, what is more fun than making a
snowman—and for this one, you don't have to wait for a snowstorm!

Creating our chubby carnation-covered snowman is a project
that kids will love to do, too. Why not make a whole gang of snowmen so your kids can give them away as presents to their teacher, say,
or to their best friends, or to grandma and grandpa when they come
to visit? At home, Holiday Snowmen make wonderful centerpieces,
with or without a tabletop forest of miniature Holiday Flower Trees,
as pictured here. For extra cheer, you might want to "wrap" up a
bunch of Fresh Flower Presents, too. You'll find them on page 133.
As we always say: Just have fun with it!®

holiday snowman

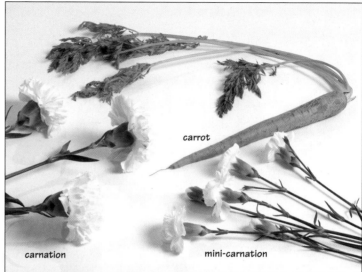

carrot

carnation

mini-carnation

Level of Difficulty: Moderate to Difficult

Time: 1 hour

Vase Life: 2 weeks

FLOWERS AND VEGETABLES

75 white carnations, 12 stems mini-carnations (to yield 62 blossoms), 1 small, clean carrot

WHAT YOU NEED

- screwdriver
- 1 drywall screw
- 4- by 3- by $\frac{1}{2}$-inch-thick block of wood
- 14- by $\frac{1}{4}$-inch diameter dowel
- glue gun and glue stick
- 7-inch-diameter plastic saucer
- sharp kitchen knife
- 1$\frac{1}{3}$ bricks of floral foam
- heavy-duty black plastic garbage bag
- 5 12-inch-long pieces of fine-gauge florist's wire
- 3 1-inch-diameter red buttons
- 2 $\frac{1}{2}$-inch-diameter black buttons
- doll's scarf and hat available at a craft store
- 2 6-inch-long twigs

1 With the screwdriver, screw the drywall screw through the block of wood into the base of the dowel. With the glue gun, hot-glue the block of wood to the plastic saucer.

2 With the kitchen knife, cut off one-third of the larger brick of floral foam. With the knife, shave off the corners of the tummy and chest pieces of floral foam. Shave the head piece so it is smaller and rounder than the chest.

3 Thoroughly soak the three chunks of floral foam in water, and place them on the black plastic bag.

4 Insert the dowel in the center of the bottom of the tummy chunk of wet floral foam; push the tummy down so that it rests on the saucer.

5 Cut all carnation stems to 2-inch lengths. Working from the bottom up, cover the floral foam tummy with large carnations (about 46) so the tummy looks round.

6 Place the foam chest on top of the tummy. Repeat Step 5 to completely cover the chest with large carnations (about 29).

Steps 1–2. Screw dowel to wooden block. Cut and shave chunks of floral foam, and soak them thoroughly.

Steps 5–6. After cutting carnations to 2-inch lengths, insert stems in each chunk of floral foam to form round head, chest, and tummy.

Steps 6–7. Push chest piece down dowel into position on tummy; repeat with snowman head.

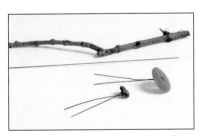

Step 8. Thread wire through each button; twist wires to secure. Set out twigs for arms.

7 Repeat Steps 5 and 6 to make the head. (You will need about 62 mini-carnations.) To give your snowman a softer, rounder look, cover the top, sides, and bottom of the chest and head, as well as the top of the tummy.

8 Thread a wire through each of the five buttons; twist the wires to secure them.

9 Insert the black eye buttons in the head of the snowman. Cut the carrot to your desired length. Wire the carrot (see page 196). Insert the carrot in the head. Tie the doll's scarf around the neck of the snowman.

10 Repeat Step 8 to position red buttons on the chest and tummy of the snowman. Add the two twigs for arms and the doll's hat.

Step 9. Insert black button eyes. Cut carrot to desired length; wire it and insert in face.

holiday charm

Joy to the world! Short days, long nights, and snowstorms often make Winter seem rather dreary, but winter, luckily, is also the season that embraces the most holidays. Revelries often begin right after Thanksgiving and last through the New Year—and even beyond. No sooner have we polished off the last of the turkey hash than up goes the Christmas tree! In fact, we know people who start putting up their decorations the day after Halloween and leave them up straight through January. That's fine with us! We love this festive season. 'Tis the season to be jolly, light the candles, wrap presents—and create and give gifts of flowers. Flowers make a huge difference in how your house will feel, adding color where there's none and fragrance, too. And, just when you think you can't stand another frost-driven cold front, here comes the most loving holiday of all— Valentine's Day, when dozens of long-stemmed roses and thoughts of love carry the day.

Berries are quite fragile, so we often mix faux berries with natural materials such as pinecones, as pictured here. If you want your wreath to last beyond the season, you can also use some silk leaves in your design. To make a wreath like this, wire bunches of berries and leaves together, then attach them to a circle made from heavy-gauge wire or a grapevine wreath. Fill in with pinecones, and keep adding more berries until the wreath is full. If you really want to use fresh berries, consider holly, winterberry, bittersweet, and cranberry— but remember, they will only last a short time.

winter greens

Evergreens seem to come into their own during the winter. All year long, we take them for granted—and then, when color fades from the countryside, they suddenly pop out in abundance. And, of course, they're wonderfully fragrant, too.

One way to enjoy evergreens is to use a lot of them in your arrangements. All year long, florists include some sort of foliage in a flower arrangement, both to frame flowers and to act as accent and filler. Foliage comes in lots of shapes and textures, from broad and glossy magnolia leaves to lustrous long-needled white pine. During the winter holidays, evergreens provide the background for many decorative arrangements, from garlands winding up banisters to swags looping across the tops of windows to wreaths hung on front doors. Not only texture, but the particular shade of green may make a difference as well. Eucalyptus, for example, has a gray-blue cast, while boxwood is glossy green.

wreath forms

Every wreath requires a solid foundation, like the heavy-gauge wire used for the magnolia wreath pictured opposite. For wreaths featuring fresh flowers and leaves, wreath-shaped floral foam works well because it can be moistened to prolong the life of your greens and blooms. For a wreath using dried materials, you might prefer using a form made of Styrofoam or compressed straw. Another option is grapevine;

Graceful Greens

Cedar–Soft sprays of needles, with overlapping scales; blue cast

False Cypress–Rich, lustrous foliage; green or with yellow or blue cast

Fir–Flat needles, bright green

Holly–Prickly, serrated-edged foliage; green or variegated; berries

Juniper–Prickly, blue cast; gray-blue berries

Eastern White Pine; Scotch Pine–Needles bundled in twos to fives; long, medium, or short

Norway Spruce; Blue Spruce–Round, four-sided needles; lose needles quickly indoors

Yew–Flat needles, green

We are so accustomed to associating pine wreaths with the holidays that we sometimes forget that many areas of the country prefer wreaths made up of other, regional materials, such as red chile peppers in the Southwest and magnolia leaves in the South. We particularly like magnolia leaves because they are so large and glossy; they are also two-toned (the back of each leaf is brown), so mixing the two colors adds visual interest to any arrangement that includes magnolia.

The easiest way to make our two-tone magnolia wreath is to wire a dozen or so separate bunches comprising two or three leaves before you begin. Make a circle of heavy-gauge wire, or bend a coat hanger into a round shape. Wire the individual bunches of leaves onto the circle, making sure to overlap them so their stems don't show. Spray your wreath with artist's fixative or hair spray, and hang it on a wall or door.

this is typically used when the vine is left exposed as part of the design. Grapevine comes in myriad sizes and shapes, including squares and hearts. It may be tightly woven or very loose. Choose the density that best suits your display. Flowers and other materials are attached to a wreath form with wire or with hot glue. Wire on the heaviest items first— then fill gaps by hot-gluing the remainder of the materials.

holiday centerpieces

Holiday tables seem positively naked if they are not decorated in some way. This is, after all, the time when we bring out our best china—either our wedding china or special holiday settings—as well as our freshly polished silver, crystal, and holiday candles. The most important part of any table design is the centerpiece, and here again, we love to go all out to make it special. A time-honored tradition is to mix fruits with flowers and greens in holiday arrangements, such as wreaths and centerpieces. Pineapple is the symbol of hospitality, so it makes a perfect focus for our Williamsburg Centerpiece, which is named for the wonderful living-history museum in Virginia.

This welcoming center-piece is dramatic and—best of all—easy! We hot-glued magnolia leaves and a chunk of floral foam to a plastic tray. Then we pierced apples with floral sticks and inserted them into the foam around the pineap-ple, along with blooming red roses. Blupernum fills in the gaps.

decorating with flowers

Holiday decorating doesn't have to follow the rules—unless you are a die-hard traditionalist and wouldn't have it any other way. What we love about Christmas and all the special occasions of the season, from skating parties to a cozy New Year's Eve dinner with friends, is giving our imaginations free rein to come up with all sorts of unexpected ideas, such as filling a stocking with flowers and hanging it on the inside of your front door or making special ornaments for the tree that include fresh flowers, such as red roses. Don't forget candles, either. From the Hanukkah menorah to simple votives flickering in the windows, candles light up the season and lend a glow that speaks to happiness and joy.

Why not welcome friends and family with a plush stocking filled with flowers? Santa may be momentarily confused, but, one glance, and even he will love the idea! Stuff your stocking with paper or other packing material, then wrap a small chunk of moist floral foam in plastic and place it on top. Cut flowers of your choice and sprigs of evergreen, and insert them into the floral foam. For a temporary design, insert roses in water tubes and place them in the stocking.

who needs ornaments?

As a spirited alternative to an ornament-and-tinsel-draped tree, why not decorate it entirely with flowers? Dried flowers are one way to go because they last indefinitely, but we prefer to blanket ours with fresh flowers, especially bright red ones such as carnations, because they look so wonderfully vibrant. Gerbera daisies are pretty because they resemble starbursts, and red roses convey an aura of romance. Mix roses that are partially opened with ones that are still in bud but are about to pop. That way they'll come to full bloom in time to welcome family for your traditional present opening and holiday meal.

Cut the stems of all the flowers to 3-inch lengths—or long enough to fit into water tubes. Cut and wind a piece of wire around each water tube, leaving the excess to hang free. Insert a flower into each tube, fill it with water, wrap stem wrap around the tube, and wire the tube to the tree. Repeat until the tree is completely covered with flowers.

For an alternative look, add or use dried flowers such as baby's breath, caspia, or statice. All look wonderful, and they obviously don't need water. You can also use these flowers fresh; place them among the boughs of the tree and let them dry naturally.

window dressing

We like to accent windows with swags that match the All-Red Flower Tree to maintain a consistent look throughout the room. Windows are your eyes on the world—but they also invite passersby to peep inside, especially during the holiday season when the tree and other decorations look so enticing.

The Window Swag rests right on top of a curtain rod; it's up to you whether or not you decide to remove your curtains or draperies. Use pruning shears to lop off greens to the correct size, and wire them to the rod with medium-gauge florist's wire. If you want a fuller look, you can hot-glue additional snips of green to the swag. Finally, attach flowers to the greens, as described in the how-to's for the All-Red Flower Tree.

a final fresh thought— roses and love!

Just when you think winter will never end, along comes one of America's favorite holidays: Valentine's Day. We love the romance of valentines and how they make people, especially our loved ones, feel special. Did you know that millions and millions of bunches of "a dozen long-stemmed roses" are purchased every Valentine's Day, not only by sweethearts for their lovers and by husbands for their wives, but also by people who simply want to connect to one another and show they care? Most people

choose red roses because they signify love. Other colors have special meanings, too, such as pink for grace and beauty, peach for charm, cream for perfection, and white for purity. If you mix red and white roses, that means you are committed to a loving relationship, and if you send one perfect rose, you are saying, "I love you!"

When you receive a gift of long-stemmed roses, you can make them last for up to 2 weeks and even longer. To do so, immerse the stems in warm water, cut off at least 1 inch of the stem at a 45-degree angle, and strip off any leaves that would lie below the water line in your vase. Fill your vase with water, and add the packet of rose food provided by your florist.

You'll want to show off your gift of roses to their best advantage, so, when massing them in a vase, position the fullest flowers at the center of the arrangement (and a few others around the rim of the vase), then fill any gaps with blooms that are not quite open. Finally, add a couple of stems bearing buds that will open later, and insert a leafy stem or two for support and textural interest.

Place your vase of roses in a prominent spot, away from heat or drafts, and change the water or floral-food solution every other day. Each time you do so, cut the stems back another inch. If a rose begins to sag, you can revive it by immersing the flower completely, head and all, in lukewarm water enriched with floral food. Leave the rose

under water until it is refreshed and firm—usually about an hour or two. Occasionally, a wilted rose requires an overnight bath to firm up completely. As time passes, you may have to change the container to accommodate the shortened stems. Teacups and perfume bottles are pretty choices for lush roses with short stems.

flower chart

The flowers and plants in this chart are ones you will find in our projects. In the wild, a number of them encompass up to 500 species; roses alone number over 4,000 varieties! Your local florist, of course, will feature only a select range of flowers in a certain number of colors. He may, however, carry many of the flowers listed below out of their so-called blooming season. Check! For more concrete information pertaining to a specific flower that you may want to include in an arrangement, consult him or your local nursery.

	FLOWER OR PLANT	AVAILABILITY	COLOR	LONGEVITY
	alstroemeria	year-round	red yellow orange cream	5 to 14 days
	amaryllis	winter/spring	red white pink salmon striped	7 to 14 days
	asparagus fern or sprengeri	year-round	green	7 days
	aster; matsumoto aster	year-round	white yellow lavender purple	7 to 14 days
	astilbe	spring	pink white lavender	5 days

FLOWER OR PLANT	AVAILABILITY	COLOR	LONGEVITY
baby's breath	year-round	white	7 to 14 days
bird-of-paradise	year-round	orange	7 to 14 days
boxwood	fall	green	months
calla lily	year-round	white purple	5 to 7 days
carnation; mini-carnation	year-round	pink red orange cream magenta white variegated	1 to 3 weeks
caspia	year-round	silvery lavender	7 to 14 days
cedar; Western red cedar	fall	green	months

(continued)

Flower or Plant	Availability	Color	Longevity
chrysanthemum; football mum	year-round	yellow, white	7 to 14 days
daffodil; also narcissus; paper white	fall/spring	yellow, salmon, cream, white, bicolor	5 to 10 days
daisy	year-round	white, yellow	7 days
delphinium	year-round	blue, pink, white, bicolor	5 to 7 days will shed flowers
eucalyptus; seeded eucalyptus	year-round	green; blue-gray leaves	1 to 3 weeks
euphorbia	winter/spring	orange, yellow, white, red	7 days

FLOWER OR PLANT	AVAILABILITY	COLOR	LONGEVITY
galax leaves	year-round	green	14 days
heather	fall/spring	pinkish-purple, purple	5 to 10 days tend to shed flowers
holly	winter	green, variegated	1 to 3 weeks
hyacinth	fall/spring	blue, violet, pink, white	5 to 10 days
hydrangea	spring	blue, violet, white	5 to 10 days
hypericum	year-round	burgundy berries	7 to 10 days
juniper	fall	green	months

(continued)

FLOWER OR PLANT	AVAILABILITY	COLOR	LONGEVITY
lemon leaves or salal leaves	year-round	green	1 to 3 weeks
lilac; French lilac	fall/spring	white, lavender	5 to 10 days water sensitive
lily; many varieties, including Asiatic lily, gloriosa lily, Oriental lily, Stargazer lily	year-round	red, yellow, orange, white, spotted, or variegated	7 to 14 days
lisianthus	year-round	*single*: white, pink, purple, red, salmon *double*: white, pink, red, salmon, bicolor	5 to 10 days
moss: sheet moss, reindeer moss, spaghnum moss, Spanish moss	year-round	varies from greenish to brownish	months
orchid; cymbidium orchid; dendrobium orchid; spray orchid	year-round	white, purple, red, lavender	7 to 14 days

FLOWER OR PLANT	AVAILABILITY	COLOR	LONGEVITY
pittosporum nigra	year-round	green, variegated	7 to 21 days
Queen Anne's lace	year-round	white	7 days
rose, thousands of varieties; spray rose	year-round	many colors; some bicolored	5 to 10 days
ruscus; Italian ruscus; Israeli ruscus	year-round	green	7 to 21 days
safflower	summer/fall	orange	months
solidago (or goldenrod)	year-round	yellow	7 to 14 days
star of Bethlehem	winter/spring	orange, white	3 to 4 weeks

(continued)

	FLOWER OR PLANT	AVAILABILITY	COLOR	LONGEVITY
	statice	year-round	pink, lavender, white	7 to 14 days
	sunflower	year-round	yellow, orange, brown, teddybear, pink	5 to 10 days
	tulip, many shapes: single, double, parrot, fringed, goblet, et cetera; French tulip	fall/spring	red, yellow, white, salmon, many colors; striped, variegated	5 to 10 days
	viburnum; snowball viburnum	winter/spring	white	10 to 14 days
	yarrow	year-round	yellow, pink, red, purple, salmon, peach	7 to 14 days

index

Boldface page references indicate photographs. *Italics* references indicate boxed text and tables or charts.

photograph credits

Maria Ferrari:

pp. 22, 46, 47, 48, 56-57, 58, 62, 66, 70, 74, 78, 82, 118, 122, 148, 149, 158, 160, 164, 168, 172, 176, 180, 204, 208, 212, 216, 220, 250.

Joseph Scafuro:

pp. 13, 15, 90, 104-105, 106, 108, 154-155, 157, 159, 200, 202, 249.

Mary and Joe Van Blerck:

pp. 2, 8, 10, 11, 12, 14, 16-17, 18, 23, 25, 28, 32, 44, 52, 55, 59, 86, 94, 98, 101, 102, 103, 107, 109, 110, 114, 128, 132, 136, 140, 144, 150, 152, 156, 184, 188, 192, 195, 201, 203, 224, 228, 232, 236, 240, 244, 247, 248, 252, 253, 254-260, and all instructional photographs.